A panto-style musical by Mark and Helen Johnson
Script by Sue Langwade

The Songs

Act One Aladdin Refrain *(repeated throughout)*
- Song 1   In The Marketplace
- Song 2   I've Had Enough
- Song 3   Some Things Go Together Perfectly
- Song 4   Just Three Wishes

Act Two
- Song 5   New Lamps For Old
- Song 6   Wishy Washy Laun-d-ry
- Song 7   I Still Believe
- Song 8   The Chase
- Song 9   Wedding Procession
- Song 10 A Panto Like No Other!

© 2014 Out of the Ark Ltd, Middlesex TW12 2HD

OH YES IT IS!
OH NO IT ISN'T!
So what is it that makes a panto, a panto?

What's the story?

People talk about the traditional pantomime, but one of the reasons this unique art form has survived for so long is its ability to adapt and encompass modern trends, whilst still retaining a structured framework. Essential to this is a strong storyline, usually adapted from a fairytale or fable, with the all-important elements of good battling evil, with good winning out in the end *(Hooray!)*. Such universal themes appeal to every generation.

Once u-pun a time...

Pantos are renowned for their abundance of corny jokes and word play (puns). The early Victorian writers took great pride in their writing and were rather scathing of the later addition of the innuendo – jokes intended to appeal to the adults in the audience and a feature which has retained its popularity to this day! You will also often find references to current affairs and contemporary culture woven into the thread of the story, ensuring an 'up to the minute' feel.

Why not see how many names of pantomime characters you can find that are 'puns'? Can you make up a few of your own?

Aladdin...tights!

Traditionally, the male lead was played by a woman. However, this trend has proved variable. Currently, the 'principal boy' is likely to be played by a Soap Star or Boy Band member, although this taste for celebrity is nothing new. At the beginning of the 20th century, the stars of pantos would have been the current music-hall favourites.

There is nothing like a Dame!

The part of the essential 'Dame' character is still taken by a man; in fact there are some actors whose whole career is spent specialising in roles such as Widow Twankey and Mother Goose! Wacky costumes, OTT make-up, a large bosom and cheeky repartee with other players and with the audience characterise these parts and no self-respecting pantomime would be without its Dame.

Making a song and dance about it!

Pantomimes often make use of popular songs, either incorporating them as they are or changing the lyrics to suit the situation. Some pantos even have a whole music score written especially for them! Hand-in-hand with the singing goes, of course, dancing. The adult singing and dancing chorus is often supplemented with local children, known as the 'juvenile' chorus or 'babes'. No panto is complete without a chorus of talented youngsters.

A play for all ages!

Panto is, first and foremost, a form of entertainment that appeals to all the family, from Great Granny to Little Sis; Dad to Uncle Joe. It is for many a first introduction to the magic of live theatre and therefore holds a special place in our hearts. Children of all ages still enjoy the time-tested routines of 'It's behind you!' and joining in with the comic song. It's good to have a place to go where age really is just a number! Long live Panto! Hooray!

CONTENTS

TEACHER'S NOTES

Synopsis	4
Song Synopsis and Performance Tips	5
Cast List	6
Staging Notes	7
Props List	8
Appendices	8
Script	9
Let Me Tell You A Story	86
Licence and Copyright Details	88

THE SONGS

	Music	Lyrics	CD Tracks
Aladdin Refrain	25	74	various
In The Marketplace	28	75	2/17
I've Had Enough	32	76	3/18
Some Things Go Together Perfectly	37	77	4/19
Just Three Wishes	40	78	7/22
New Lamps For Old	44	79	9/24
Wishy Washy Laun-d-ry	50	80	10/25
I Still Believe	54	81	12/27
The Chase	59	82	13/28
Wedding Procession	66	84	14/29
A Panto Like No Other!	70	85	15/30

Keep an eye on our website (www.outoftheark.com) for updates and resources for this, and all our other publications.

SYNOPSIS

Set within the context of the 1001 Arabian Nights from which the story originates, this panto-style version of Aladdin contains all the traditional elements and characters, alongside a whole host of less conventional ones!

The opening catchy refrain, *Aladdin, Aladdin* serves as a commentary on the action and is repeated throughout the whole play. We then enter the bustling, spice-fragranced Eastern streets and encounter dancers, musicians and pickpockets through the lively rhythms of the opening number *In The Market Place*. Here we meet the hero of our play, Aladdin, a kind-hearted lad determined to build a new village hall for his community *(Hooray!)*. There is hissing and booing at the wicked Abanazar, who aims to find the long-lost Lamp of Unlimited Power, destroy the village completely and replace it with a dazzling resort for the rich and famous – and Ofsted inspectors *(More hissing & booing!)*.

On the other side of town, we see the frustration of the lovely Princess Jasmine, trapped in a life of luxury at the Palace, as she expresses her innermost thoughts in the pacy solo song *I've Had Enough*. Jasmine, disguised as a commoner, relishes an all-too-brief escape into the outside world before allowing us a glimpse at the wonder of emerging love when she meets Aladdin and they reveal their feelings in the amusing duet *Some Things Go Together Perfectly*. Abanazar then attempts to thwart their love and use Aladdin for his own evil purposes before abandoning him in a deep, dark cave! But fate favours Aladdin and he there encounters the magical Genie of the Lamp, who, along with his assistants *The Three Wishes*, shows Aladdin what the future could hold for him in the upbeat, feel-good song *Just Three Wishes*. Act One closes with Aladdin now rich enough to marry his love! *(Hooray!)*

Act Two begins with a joyous proposal before the devious Abanazar works out another cunning plan in the potently enticing rhythm of *New Lamps For Old* and (horror of horrors) finally gains the power he has craved! We are treated to a welcome moment of comic relief as Aladdin's mother, Widow Twankey, and his twin brothers Wishy and Washy sing the wonderfully comic number *Wishy Washy Laun-d-ry*.

Reach for the hankies yet again as Abanazar cruelly separates our young lovers, yet we are still encouraged to cling to a brave hope that all may work out in the touching ballad duet *I Still Believe*. Their faith proves to be well founded as once more the tables turn and Widow Twankey gets back the lamp *(Hooray!)*.

We continue on the roller-coaster ride towards a conclusion with Aladdin, Jasmine and her father pursuing Widow Twankey through the streets with Abanazar and his guards hot on their trail. All this to the increasingly hectic strains of *The Chase*, which thankfully ends satisfactorily with Aladdin being restored to good fortune.

The audience then participates as part of the congregation to celebrate the marriage of Aladdin and Jasmine, in the calm and solemn *Wedding Procession*. Finally, who can resist the urge to clap hands and stamp feet to the perfect finale song *A Panto Like No Other!* as the cast and crew enjoy a well-deserved moment of glory?

SONG SYNOPSIS and PERFORMANCE TIPS

ALADDIN REFRAIN [All]
This short and catchy refrain provides a running commentary on the action, appearing with different lyrics at five key points throughout the performance. (The backing track could also be used for scene changes or at the end of Act One.)

IN THE MARKETPLACE [All]
This lively shuffle-style song launches us into a bustling and animated market scene where we meet Aladdin. Easy to learn and full of life, it has been written with bags of scope for dramatisation. Look out for the 6/8 sections for specific acting ideas featuring pick-pockets and overloaded market traders.

I'VE HAD ENOUGH [Jasmine and All]
Mostly a solo for the frustrated Jasmine, but with vocal support throughout. This song requires a good dose of 'strop' and confidence as she expresses her desire to be free. Great fun to sing with opportunities for acting from her maids.

SOME THINGS GO TOGETHER PERFECTLY [Duet for Jasmine and Aladdin, All support]
This is our 'boy-meets-girl-in-the-market' song. Light-hearted, jazzy and easy to sing. A duet for Jasmine and Aladdin, with everyone joining in on the chorus. Plentiful vegetable props will only help with the flavour of the song.

JUST THREE WISHES [Genie, The Three Wishes, Brass Section, All]
This upbeat 'ska' song is a lot of fun, giving scope for big choreography from The Three Wishes backing singers, and the Genie's 'Madness'-style brass section. Baggy trousers optional!

NEW LAMPS FOR OLD [Abanazar, 3 Groups]
A spellbinding melody with a sinister twist. Abanazar outworks his evil plan to recover the lamp. Each of the three parts that the villain introduces is taken up by the crowds, building into an irresistible offer and a very satisfying song.

WISHY WASHY LAUN-D-RY [Widow Twankey, Wishy, Washy, All]
A larger-than-life, colourful number that should have the audience in stitches. Does lend itself to some garish and outrageous 'laundry' props. Worth a little work on articulation in the chorus to help deliver this OTT panto song with maximum impact.

I STILL BELIEVE [Aladdin, Jasmine, All]
The big ballad duet for Aladdin and Jasmine, in the face of interrupted love and impending doom at the hands of Abanazar. Sung from opposite sides of the stage – both parts interweave, with vocal support in the choruses/bridge. This song needs plenty of conviction in its delivery (and 'lighter' waving from the audience). Keep the tissues handy!

THE CHASE [3 Groups of 3]
Based on *The Hall of the Mountain King* from the *Peer Gynt Suite No.1* by Grieg, this song is shared by three main groups, with scope for the odd solo line. From a tentative, whispered start, through to a frenzied crescendo, *The Chase* should provide bags of fun and maximum entertainment. Careful choreography will pay dividends.

WEDDING PROCESSION [All, in 3 parts]
This reverent, solemn song brings a serious note, with the audience becoming the wedding guests. A little unusual to have a song like this in a panto perhaps, but it does allow space for pause and reflection and provides a good balance to the previous and following songs.

A PANTO LIKE NO OTHER! [All]
This upbeat, lively tune brings the show to a rousing conclusion and gives all the cast a chance to join together on stage. This is the song that likes to say thank you to all involved. Have your collection hats at the ready! (There is a condensed, faster version *(CD track 38)* to allow the cast to exit the stage. The backing track *(CD track 30)* could also be used as a final curtain call.)

CAST LIST

Speaking parts (*denotes solo/duet singing also):

Scheherazade	*a tale teller (in the best possible way!)*
Sultan	*required to look grumpy; enjoys chopping heads off (an easy part to cast)*
Sultan's Servant	*a lyrical lad/lass*
Aladdin*	*our ragged hero with a heart of gold*
Widow Twankey*	*a larger-than-life character with an eccentric style of dress*
Wishy / Washy	*Aladdin's inseparable twin brothers*
Abanazar*	*he's bad!*
Wantu	*the evil sidekick with a rhyming compulsion*
12 villagers/tradespeople	*hard-working people, the heart and soul of the village (lines can be doubled up if fewer parts are required)*
Wife	*Villager 4's other half*
Builder	*Mr Brick*
King	*Jasmine's father, a right royal collector*
Jasmine*	*our lovely heroine who just wants to break free*
King's Servants x 3	*a better class of servant*
Suitors x 4	*hopefuls for Jasmine's hand in marriage*
Jasmine's Maids x 3*	*girlies*
Oracle	*wise guardian of the Cave of Wonders; stony expression*
Man / Woman	*typical married couple*
Trader	*a sweet person*
Washing Line x 2	*supporting roles*
Genie*	*the dispenser of wishes (with a touch of madness)*
The Three Wishes*	*Genie's female backing singers*
Tom	*the flying carpet (with mat nav)*
Gems x 4	*priceless parts*
DJ	*a sultry voice with a face for radio*
Matt Paint / Wal Paper	*a decorative pair*
Mr Rick / Mr Shaw	*moving parts*
Salesman	*slick*
PC Bright / PC Crook	*the long arms of the law*
Police	*arresting roles*
Rats x 2	*rodent heroes*
MC	*an upstanding character part*

Non-speaking parts

Gong Hitter	*bound to be a resounding success*
Non-speaking suitors	*strong, silent types (see Appendices, p8 for list of suitable suitors)*

Essential others

Chief Cardholder/s	*audience autocue operator/s*

If additional parts are required, these groups can be augmented:

Non-speaking police	*arresting looks only*
Non-speaking villagers	*keep their thoughts to themselves*

STAGING NOTES

Although at first sight there are a number of scenes in this production, they can be represented fairly simply by using a generic Eastern village as a backdrop and having side 'flats' (large dividers can be handy), at either side of the stage, stage left (SL)* being the Palace side and stage right (SR) the 'Seedy side of town' with paintings of a palace/some run-down shops respectively. If you want to have several different visuals, you can pin various scenes to the back of the 'flats' and 'throw' them over as required. Heavy-duty white sheeting or very large, sturdy paper can be used for this.

Alternatively, include the launderette and palace on the village backdrop and use signs and a few well-chosen props to denote the various scenes.

If you want to include some shops on your backdrop, the following are suggestions for some silly names:

- Rex Carz Automobile repairs
- Lee King & Ray D Ator Central heating specialists
- Bill Board Advertising
- Ted E. Bares Toy Shoppe
- Kareem Cheese Deli
- Chester Drawers quality furniture

Keep an eye on the Out of the Ark website (www.outoftheark.com) for any digital backdrops that may become available for this musical.

Other possible signs and ideas to set the different scenes:

The Desert

'The Desert: Nearest Oasis 10 km (Picture of a camel/fork and spoon/KFC)**'**

You could also have a couple of children wafting some sand-coloured fabric on the front of the stage

The Palace

'The Palace: A cross between Buckingham Palace and the *(local Eastern restaurant)***'**

Add a couple of throne-like chairs and an eastern-type rug. If you can find a stuffed corgi or two, all the better!

The Palace – Jasmine's Room

'Jasmine's room: Only girls allowed'

Keep this the same as the palace, but throw some clothes on the thrones/floor and put up a One Direction poster.

The Launderette

'The Launderette: Your stain's our gain!'

Act One: carry on a table with tub, powder (value/essentials range), etc. and laundry baskets/bags with signs on, as per stage directions. The washing line will be carried on.

Act Two: powder should now be 'Waitrose/Tesco Finest'; washing machine is brought on.

Inside the Cave of Wonders

'The Cave of Wonders: Nothing under £1,000!'

Low lighting would be useful for this scene and you will definitely need some treasure.

---

* Stage left is the actor's left as they stand on the stage facing the audience, similarly, stage right is the actor's right as they face the audience.

PROPS CHECKLIST

Prompt cards:
- [ ] Ahh!; Hooray!; BOO!; Groan!; BOO! HISS!; Much later; Visual thumbs up & down; Yes

Smaller props:
- [ ] Vegetables
- [ ] Box containing a brick, PVA glue, photo suitable for dartboard
- [ ] Small gong
- [ ] Apples
- [ ] Newspaper for Sultan: 'Rotten Rulers Weekly – Why beheading your wife may be the best way to cut your losses'
- [ ] Book for Scheherazade: 'Coming soon, 1001 Arabian Nights'
- [ ] List and scroll for Abanazar
- [ ] Chair
- [ ] Apple peeling (could be spiral of green paper)
- [ ] Trumpet (real or 2D)
- [ ] Scroll for servant
- [ ] Hairbrush, powder, etc. for Jasmine's Maids
- [ ] Bags of sweets
- [ ] Perfume bottle
- [ ] Rope
- [ ] Lamp
- [ ] Brass instruments (real or 2D)
- [ ] Certificates
- [ ] Signposts: 'To Wishy Washy Laundry'; 'To New Village Hall'
- [ ] String of lamps
- [ ] Box of junk (which will have lamp on top in Act 2)
- [ ] Gems for Aladdin
- [ ] DJ Headphones
- [ ] Bag with bloomers etc. in for Widow T to show Abanazar
- [ ] Paper for rats

Larger props:
- [ ] Rickshaw (use a cut cardboard box for the frame of the 'car' with handles on the inside of this. Attach a wooden frame to the outside and cardboard wheels)
- [ ] Signs for rear of rickshaw 'Heavy Load on board' 'UR 2 WED' and balloons
- [ ] Washing machine
- [ ] Stalls for market traders with suitable items
- [ ] Washing line with odd socks, humorous items
- [ ] Bags for launderette with contemporary references
- [ ] Treasure for cave
- [ ] Decorator's van (Matt Paint and Wal Paper, Superior Decorators, watching paint dry since 1990) Could be 2D or cardboard box with shoulder straps that one of them could be 'wearing'

APPENDICES

Alternative suitors (non-speaking)

Name	Comment	Costume/prop
Otto Graph	thinks a lot of himself	celebrity
Hugh Canduit	an encouraging character	carrying sign 'You go girl!'
Olaf Atdejoke	a bit miserable	dark outfit, miserable face
Al Gebrah	a bit of a mystery man	spy outfit
Dick Shanary	self explanatory	just wave
Theo Saurus	smart, intelligent, clever, bright	'boffin' outfit
Dan Druff	a bit flaky	scratching head
Earl E Byrd	worms his way into your affections	plumed hat and worm
Emile Ticket	rich and foolish	posh outfit
Marcus Absent	never around when you want him	doesn't appear
Lee Derhosen	eccentric dresser	lederhosen!
Harry Stockracy	a cut above the rest	country gent, royal wave

Alternative Suitors (Speaking)

I'll take you up mountains, through jungles and nettles,
You'll just need a rucksack, insect spray and a kettle.
Explorer outfit

Let me cook you up banquets, TV dinners and roasts,
Be the hostess with the mostest and I'll be your host!
Chef

You'll tremble at my tremolo; at my quavers you will quiver
My virtuoso vibrato down your spine will make you shiver!
Opera singer

SCRIPT

ACT ONE

Scene 1: THE VILLAGE

A village set is already on stage. If you choose to add signs, the Launderette is off SR (Stage Right) and the Palace SL (Stage Left). There is a box marked: 'Build the Village Hall Fund', containing a brick, some PVA glue and a photo of a relevant personality, positioned at the side of the stage. The Cardholder(s) will need to be seated at one side of the stage.

SFX Wedding Bells — CD Track 31

As the Wedding Bells are heard, Scheherazade, Sultan and servant/s enter, preferably through audience. Scheherazade and Sultan sit at side of stage throughout, watching the action.

Sultan Why have you brought apples? They're green!

Servant As green as the glint in a jealous suitor's eye, your eminence! As you requested yesterday, they were transported from France.

Sultan That was yesterday! Today I hate green! Bring me oranges!

Servant I am as happy to do your bidding as musical notes are to be part of a divine melody! *(Exit)*

Scheherazade moves front of stage. Sultan could be reading a large newspaper, 'Rotten Rulers Weekly – Why beheading your wife can be the best way to cut your losses'. Scheherazade could have her words in a book with the title: 'Coming Soon 1001 Arabian Nights'.

Scheherazade I am Scheherazade, the Sultan's new bride.
All of his others have suddenly died!
After the wedding, no breakfast in bed –
She says, 'I do', he says, 'Off with her head!'
If **I'm** to survive for **more** than one **night**
I must weave **tales** for the **Sul**tan's de**light**.
Stories alive with in**tri**gue and ro**mance** –
To **keep** him en**thralled** is my only **chance!**
(Thinks for a moment or two) I know! A panto!
Heroes and baddies, humour and drama!
A beauty; a lad – how will he charm her?
At first his clothes may be all in tatters,
But is his heart kind? That's what really matters.
Imagine a market, vibrant with life,
Teeming with people – from Lord to fishwife.
A suitable setting, full of mystique,
All kinds of people are crowding the streets!

Villagers start to enter from both sides of stage.

Let the action begin, my story unfold,
It had better be good, his int'rest to hold *(indicating Sultan)*.
So, do please join in to help move it along,
Ah, here comes our hero! Bring on the gong!

Gong Hitter carries on small gong and taps it as...

SFX Loud Gong — CD Track 32

Gong Hitter shakes then exits. Aladdin enters looking tatty and rather dirty, carrying some vegetables, with which he could be juggling/playing around.

ALADDIN REFRAIN 1 *(See p74 for lyrics)* — CD Track 1/16

Aladdin	Hello everyone! My name's Aladdin – Aladdin muddy trousers! Good job my mum runs the local launderette. I've come to sell these vegetables at the market, to make some money towards the Build a Village Hall fund! I work in the Palace Gardens you see and they let me take these as part of my wages. Let's see what we've got so far. *(Looking in box)* One brick, well that's a start, I suppose.
Builder	*(Taking brick)* So that's where that went. At last I can finish my extension!
Aladdin	Some PVA glue – that always comes in handy. Especially in sticky situations! And a photo of *(Appropriate name, e.g. Michael Gove)*. What's that for?
Villager 1	Oh, that's to go on the dartboard!
Aladdin	Oh dear, we're not doing very well, are we? We'll just have to keep trying. You see, boys and girls, I **really** want to be an entertainer, but there's nowhere to put on shows at the moment!

Cue Card: Ahh!

And everybody knows how important shows are!

Cue Card: Hooray!

Don't worry, we'll get there! Times might be tough, *(All nod miserably)* but we're all in it together! *(All smile)* So come on, let's get this market started!

Villager 1	Apricots, the juiciest in all the east!
Villager 2	Spice up your life! Fragrant spices from the far corners of the kingdom!
Villager 3	Fabrics that can transform even the plainest weed into an exotic bloom!
Villager 4	I'll have ten metres for my wife!
Wife	*(Hitting him with bag)* Oi! Don't be cheeky, you distant cousin of a gnat!

SONG 1   IN THE MARKETPLACE *(see p75 for lyrics)*   CD Track 2/17

Throughout the song, the stage needs to be a bustling scene, with the various characters mentioned in the lyrics appearing at the relevant moment, i.e. dancers, musicians, etc. It would be fun to have some pickpockets who sneak across the stage during the Chorus, plying their trade!

Abanazar enters SL.   *Cue Card: BOO! HISS!*

Abanazar	*(Pushing villagers)* Out of my way, you slimy drippings from a camel's nose!

Villagers move to BOS (back of stage) in groups and mime grumbling. Abanazar moves FOS (front of stage) and addresses the audience.

Abanazar	**I** am the keen edge of a tiger's tooth; the sneer which plays on a hyena's lips. **I** am Abanazar, Grand Vizier to the Emperor, soon to be Master of the Universe!
	I finally have this ancient scroll, you see, telling me where to find the Lamp of Unlimited Power! When I have that lamp, I will take over the land, banish all the villagers to a life of hard labour and build a resort and golf course for the ridiculously rich and famous and Ofsted inspectors. *Cue Card: BOO!*
	I'll wipe the smiles off the faces of these cheeky peasants who show me no respect! When I have the lamp they'll throw themselves on my mercy – and it'll be a hard landing because I haven't got any! Ha, ha, ha! *Cue Card: BOO! HISS!*
	Now where is my lazy sidekick? Wantu! Wantu!
Wantu	*(Running on SL)* Three, four, shake your booty on the floor! *(Does silly dance)*
Abanazar	Wantu! Have I ever told you, you are the most irritating, evil sidekick ever?
Wantu	Twice a day and sometimes three! I annoy you constantly!
Abanazar	*(To audience)* When he was a young scrap he was caught in a mystic moonbeam at midnight and ever since has spoken only in rhyme.

Wantu	When I speak, I speak in rhyme, I try not to… but it happens every time!
Abanazar	*(Aside)* That'll teach me to go to 'Sidekicks R Us' for an evil accomplice. I should have gone somewhere posh like 'Horrids'. But when I get the lamp, I'll find a sidekick who's more genteel, then I'll be the slinkiest slither of the slipperiest eel! D'oh, this rhyming thing is catching! Wantu! Come with me!
Wantu	*(To audience)* Of course I 'wantu' go with him – not! **No** choice is the only one I've got!

Abanazar and Wantu exit. Villagers drift forward again.

Villager 5	Mangoes! Succulent mangoes!
Aladdin	Hey! That reminds me of my favourite joke! **Man goes** to the Doctor's with a strawberry growing out of his head. The Doctor says, 'I'll give you some cream for that!' *(All laugh)* I love that joke!
Villager 6	Hi Aladdin! I've got a good joke for you! What's the fastest vegetable?
All	We don't know. What is the fastest vegetable?
Village 6	A runner bean!
Aladdin	Thanks! That's great! I'll put it in my routine on opening night!
Villager 5	It'll be great to have somewhere we can put on shows and have belly-dancing classes.
Villager 7	And Zumba™, mother and toddler, Senior Moves*[1]…
Villager 6	… and support groups for retired teachers. *(All agree)*
Aladdin	Oh, I think I can feel the ground shaking. That must be my mum!

Enter Widow Twankey SR.

Widow T	Aladdin! Yoo hoo! *(Spotting audience)* Oh, hello boys and girls! I didn't know you had so many friends, Aladdin. Those PSHCE lessons must really be working! And they all look very intelligent. Now, I'm trying to think of a new name for my launderette but I can't think of anything I like. Maybe your friends could help. *(To audience)* Could you give a 'thumbs up' if you like our suggestions and a 'thumbs down' if you don't?

Widow Twankey and Aladdin pace and think, then suggest ideas. The Cardholder holds up relevant signs with a visual cue.

Aladdin	'Suds-u-like'? *(Widow T shakes head)*	Cue Card: 👎
Widow T	'Squeaky-clean laundry'? *(Aladdin shakes his head)*	Cue Card: 👎
Aladdin	Wash your problem? *(Widow T shakes head)*	Cue Card: 👎
Widow T	Have you seen your twin brothers, Wishy and Washy? Maybe they could help.	
Aladdin	Hey! That would be a good name, the Wishy Washy Laundry! Wow! They like it too! Come on, I'll give you a hand making the sign, Mum.	Cue Card: 👍
Widow T	Oh you are a good boy, helping out a damsel in distress!	

Widow T and Aladdin exit SR.

Villager 9	*(Moving downstage, to audience)* I don't know about a damsel in **dis**tress! In **dat** dress she looks more like a camel!

All exit.

---

1. *Throughout the script, * equals possible product placement opportunity. (This can be a useful fundraising idea, perhaps using held-up cue cards. Alternatively, space can be offered on the programme for relevant local businesses.)*

Scene 2: THE PALACE

There needs to be at least one chair at the side of the stage. Enter King SL, carrying apple peeling and accompanied by 3 servants – one with a trumpet, one with a long scroll.

King *(To servant, holding up apple peeling)* Who do you think this looks like?

Servant 1 *(Uncertainly)* Er, we don't all have your artistic imagination, Your Highness.

King It's obvious! It's *(insert name)* Add it to my 'apple peelings that look like famous people' collection. Put it next to *(Cruella de Vil)*. There are certain similarities.

Servant 1 *(To audience)* Apple peelings that look like famous people indeed! He's barmy to the **core**!

Cue Card: Groan!

King I don't know what I'd do without my collection of collections. With all the things I have to worry about, it's the only thing that keeps me sane! You haven't seen my marbles collection have you? I seem to have lost it somewhere.

Servant 1 No, sorry Your Highness! *(Exits as Jasmine enters SL)*

King Ah! My beautiful daughter! Now, Jasmine, as it's almost your birthday, we must think about the ancient law regarding your marriage. *(To servant with scroll)* Read it to me.* *(It was prepared by... Solicitors)*

Servant 2 Any Princess not wishing to be exiled to the Island of Beastly Beetles and Crawling Creepies must marry before the birthday specified on page 902, Paragraph 9, Clause b. She must marry a man who is preferably of good character, possibly with a title, but who absolutely must have **loads of** money and look good in glossy magazines. For further details, see page 306, paragraph 17.

King So, my dear, I have arranged for a selection of suitable suitors to come here so you can choose a husband. Isn't that exciting?

Jasmine Father, I know you only want the best for me but I don't think I can do this! I want to be free to marry someone I fall in love with!

King You are, Jasmine! You're free to fall in love with any one of them! Servant, please announce them! *(He claps)*

As each is announced, SFX: Off-key trumpet fanfare *(CD track 33), mimed by Servant 2. The suitors walk slowly across the stage giving a royal wave, then exit.*

Servant 3 Prince Boris of London! *(Enter Prince with wild blond hairdo)*
(Aside) He doesn't need a wife, he needs a hairdresser!

Prince Alarming of Transylvania! *(Pale with blood-red lips)*
(Aside) Not a **fang**tastic match, if you ask me.

Duke Humeer of Tenn *(D'you come 'ere often? Spivvy looking character)*
(Aside) Bit of a dubious **pun**-ter!

For further suggestions, see list of other suitable suitors in Appendices, p8

Cue Card: Much later

Jasmine sits looking very bored. Four more suitors stand/sit at one side of the stage, stepping forward one at a time. Again, for further suggestions see list in Appendices (p8).

Suitor 1 I'm fit, handsome and charming, you lucky Princess,
Watch my cool gym moves and you'll be impressed! *(Action)*

Suitor 2 The most lavish wedding I will arrange,
I could buy a small country with just my loose change! *(Rattles coins)*

Suitor 3 With me you can tap dance into the sunset,
There's nothing to rival my shuffle hop step!
(Short tap sequence. Optional VO: Seven!)

Suitor 4	I'm a footballing genius and I need a wag! To go with my big house and ten vintage jags.
Jasmine	*(Jumping up)* I've had enough! Father, I'm grateful you've gone to so much effort and thank you all for coming but you've had a wasted journey! *(She runs off)*
King	*(To suitors)* Why don't we all go and have a look at my collections and give the Princess a chance to calm down? *(Exit)*

Jasmine re-enters with maids, who are carrying various cosmetics, hairbrushes, etc.

Jasmine	I hate being a princess! It's not fair! Why can't I just live an ordinary life?
Maid 1	Don't be too keen to give up being royal, being ordinary's not all that!

SONG 2   I'VE HAD ENOUGH *(See p76 for lyrics)*   CD Track 3/18
[Jasmine]

During the song, the maids could attempt to brush Jasmine's hair, powder her nose, etc. but she keeps pushing them away as she paces around the stage in an agitated fashion.

Maid 2	Every life has its ups and downs, Princess, you just have to look on the bright side.
Maid 3	The grass always looks greener on the other side until you get there and realize there are weeds in there as well.
Jasmine	If only I could be free, even for one day!
Maid 1	I know! Why don't you swap clothes with one of us, just for a little while? You could sneak out to the market and we'll cover for you.
Jasmine	Do you really think I could?
Maid 2	Why not? You could bring us all back some sweets – there's a really good stall in the market.
Maid 3	Come on! We've got to make a princess into a commoner – a kind of Cinderella in reverse!

All exit SL.

Scene 3: THE DESERT

SFX Desert Wind   CD Track 34

The Oracle enters and stands SR facing audience with head bowed and eyes closed. Enter Abanazar and Wantu SL. Abanazar has a large scroll.

Abanazar	At last, the entrance to the Cave of Wonders! I believe the Lamp of Unlimited Power lies within! Let me unroll the ancient scroll which gives me the special words to move away this mighty rock. 1 packet of Haribo, 4 pairs of superman boxer shorts, 1 box Grecian 2000 for men...* *(Special offer from...)* Pah! That's my shopping list. Ah! Here it is! *(Clears his throat)* I, the great and mighty Abanazar, demand entry to the wonderful world of this curious cave!
Oracle	*(Lifting up head and opening eyes)* Good day, A bandana! Never mind the alliteration, what are the magic words?
Abanazar	*(Annoyed, reading)* **Please** and **thank you!** Aha! That should have done it, now roll over, Rocky!
Wantu	My imagination can stretch quite far, But I can't see my master as a **rock** and **roll** star!

Abanazar stretches his hand towards Oracle's metal ring.

Oracle	*(Slapping his hand away)* **You** cannot enter here, Have-a-Nana! Only one who is truly kind and pure of heart can do that.
Abanazar	It's **Abanazar**, you gormless granite; you senseless stone!
Oracle	*(Annoyed)* Well, it must be one called **Aladdin**. And anyone who resorts to calling nasty names doesn't deserve any help, isn't that right, boys and girls? *Cue Card: Yes!*
	Goodbye Ebenezer! *(Closes eyes and bows head)*
Abanazar	Bah! May the smell of sweaty PE kits be ever in your nostrils! Come on, Wantu, you nincompoop's knicker elastic! Let's go and see if we can find 'Aladdin waiting'. Waiting for us to seal his fate! *Cue Card: BOO! HISS!*
Wantu	Bye bye! Must fly!

They exit SL, followed by Oracle.

Scene 4: THE MARKETPLACE

Enter villagers (including a married couple), traders, one sweet stall and stall holder. Jasmine enters, looking around, fascinated.

Villager 10	Buy your plums, 2 cartons for the price of 1! *(To Jasmine)* Would you like to try one darlin'?
Jasmine	Oh, thank you very much!
Villager 11	Perfume! Special offer today only! *(To couple)* Would you like a little squirt?
Woman	*(Indicating husband)* I've already got one thanks!
Villager 11	*(To Jasmine)* How about you? Make you smell like a princess!

She squirts Jasmine as Aladdin enters. He and Jasmine both make the same 'phew!' gesture from the bad perfume smell, and hold their noses (not facing each other) then they both head for the sweet stall.

Jasmine & Al	I'd like some of those please, they're my favourite! *(Noticing each other)* Jinx! *(Both laugh)*
Trader	A bag for you and a bag for you! *(They each take and hand over money)* Anyone else? * *(Sweetshop)*
Man	*(Indicating wife)* I've already got a bag!
Villager 5	Mangoes! Get the finest mangoes here!
Jasmine	Hey! That reminds me of my favourite joke! **Man goes** into the Doctor's with a strawberry growing out of his head and the Doctor says, 'I'll give you some cream for that.' *(Both laugh)* I love that joke!
Aladdin	So do I! Are you new around here? I don't remember seeing you before.
Jasmine	Er, I've come from the Palace.
Aladdin	You work at the Palace? So do I, in the gardens. But I really want to be an entertainer. Listen, how do you make an artichoke?
Jasmine	I don't know, how do you make an artichoke?
Aladdin	You strangle it! *(Both laugh)*
Jasmine	What's small, round and giggles a lot?
Aladdin	I don't know. What's small, round and giggles a lot?
Jasmine	A tickled onion! *(Both laugh)*
Aladdin	Hey, we could be a double act!

SONG 3 SOME THINGS GO TOGETHER PERFECTLY   CD Track 4/19
(See p77 for lyrics) [Jasmine/Aladdin]

During this song it would be fun to have pairs/groups of children dancing as the various foodstuffs are mentioned. Aladdin and Jasmine could join them in a sequence of actions during the chorus. At the end of the song, Al and Jasmine mime chatting. Abanazar enters SL with Wantu limping behind. They move across to SR.

Abanazar Wantu, keep up, you lazy lizard's nail clippings!

Wantu All right! I can't go much faster,
These shoes hurt – I need a plaster.* *(Local chemist)*

Abanazar waits impatiently at far side of stage, while one of the villagers mimes giving Wantu a plaster for his foot. Jasmine spots Abanazar and begins to hurry away.

Jasmine *(Exiting SL, trying to hide her face)* I must go, my... *(pauses)* mistress will be wondering where I am. Goodbye!

Abanazar *(Aside)* Ha! If I'm not mistaken that's Princess Jasmine!

Aladdin *(Calling after her)* Goodbye! My name's Aladdin! You can find me at Widow Twankey's Launderette if you'd like to! *(To villagers)* Hey! Did you happen to see the most beautiful girl in the world?

He exits dreamily SR.

Abanazar Aladdin! What a stroke of luck! And it looks as if he's 'Aladdin love' – with the Princess. *(Thinks)* Aha! I'll tell him who his love really is and then offer him the chance to get rich so that he can marry her.   Cue Card: Ahh!

Wantu *(To audience)* Don't get sentimental, they won't make it to the church,
Abanazar will just use him and then leave him in the lurch!

They exit SR.

ALADDIN REFRAIN 2 *(See p74 for lyrics)*   CD Track 5/20

Scene 5: WIDOW TWANKEY'S LAUNDERETTE

There could be some bags of laundry labelled with reference to current affairs, e.g. 'Freshly Laundered Money: The Vatican'; 'Dirty Laundry c/o Chat Magazine'. If you have a child's small suit or two, they could be labelled 'For Ant and Dec'. You get the idea! However, beware not to cause offence!

Two people hold up a washing line hung with lots of odd socks and any other humorous items you have to hand. Widow T has a washing bowl with oversized pair of bloomers in and washboard, if poss.

Wash Line 1 When the teacher said we'd have important supporting roles, this wasn't what we thought s/he meant!

Wash Line 2 Yeah! 'Supporting roles involving some long and colourful lines!' Huh! Never trust a teacher!

Widow T *(Miming doing washing in bowl)* Swishy, swashy, swishy, swashy!

Wishy and Washy enter.

W&W *(Together)* Did you call us, Mummy wummy?

Widow T Hello Wishy, hello Washy! Have you come to give me a hand? Wring out Mr/s _____ bloomers, would you? Could take a while. *(Hands them bloomers)*

Wishy Easy peasy

Washy Lemon squeezy! *(They mime wringing them out)*

Widow T And look at all these odd socks! Anyone would think I had a centipede with cold feet for a customer! *(Wiping her brow)* Ooh, it's so steamy and full of hot air in here, it's just like a staffroom at lunchtime.

Abanazar enters, in disguise.

Abanazar	Ding dong, anybody home?
Widow T	Widow Twankey at your service. What can I do you for?
Abanazar	*(Bowing)* Madame *(Reaction from Widow T)*, what can **I** do for you? I am your long lost brother-in-law; your late husband's brother.
Widow T	My husband didn't have a brother! He was a **lonely** child!
Abanazar	*(Condescendingly)* You mean he was an **only** child.
Widow T	Aha! So you admit it, he didn't have a brother!
Abanazar	Oh yes he did!
Widow T	Oh no he didn't!... *(Etc., until...)*
Abanazar	Oh yes he did and now I'm here with a job for my nephew, Aladdin. He will be richly rewarded.
Widow T	Why didn't you say? But sadly, you've just missed him. He went off to write lovesick poetry. Why not take Wishy and Washy instead?
W&W	*(Shaking hands)* B-O-G-O-F!
Abanazar	I beg your pardon!
Wishy	Buy one...
Washy	...Get one free!
Abanazar	I'm sure I'll find a task for this charming pair, but for now I need Aladdin.
Widow T	Righto! I'll send him as soon as he gets back. Where do you live?
Abanazar	Just tell him to meet me on the edge of town, near the great rock at the gateway to the Desolate Desert.
Widow T	Just past Tesco's?
Abanazar	That's right.
Wishy	Super.
Washy	Duper!

All exit SR.

Scene 6: INSIDE THE CAVE OF WONDERS

SFX: Spooky Atmosphere *(Gradually fade out)* CD Track 35

Abanazar stands at the side of stage SR, holding the end of a rope. Wantu stands behind him. There should be some treasure set on stage, including the Lamp of Unlimited Power. Gems need to be curled up at the back of the stage. As Scheherazade and Abanazar speak, Aladdin should enter slowly, through audience if possible, as though walking in a very dark place. When he arrives at the treasure, he mimes looking through it and finds the lamp.

Scheherazade	As the next scene is unfolding, let me bring you up to speed, Abanazar sought Aladdin's help and our Al has agreed! For love of Princess Jasmine, he'll do anything he can To make sure that he's qualified to be her lifetime man. Can't you feel the tension mounting now our Al's taken the bait? If you want to see what happens, there isn't long to wait!
Abanazar	At last I have 'Aladdin the cave'! I have lowered him down and pulled up the rope so as soon as he throws me the lamp, I'll close up the entrance and leave him to perish! Oh, it's so much fun being mean!

Cue Card: BOO! HISS!

Wantu	*(Popping out from behind)* You can see my master's truly rotten! *(Disappears, then after a short pause, pops back up)* If you're waiting for the rhyme – I haven't forgotten!
Aladdin	Uncle, I've found the lamp, please throw me the rope!
Abanazar	Throw me the lamp first, so you'll have both hands free.
Aladdin	I'll manage. Throw me the rope!
Abanazar	The lamp!
Aladdin	The rope!
Abanazar	The lamp!
Aladdin	The rope!
Wantu	*(Popping out)* Abanazar won't let him exit In case he takes the lamp and legs it!
Abanazar	*(To Aladdin)* You maggot in the apple of my life! Stay there for a few hours and think about it! *(To audience)* I'll go to my tailor and get him started on my Master of the Universe outfit! When I come back, he'll be begging me to take the lamp off him – ha, ha, ha!

Cue Card: BOO! HISS!

Exit Abanazar and Wantu.

ALADDIN REFRAIN 3 *(See p74 for lyrics)*   CD Track 6/21

SFX: Spooky Atmosphere *(Gradually fade as before)*   CD Track 35

Aladdin	It's scary in here! It's so dark. * *(You should have gone to... (Lighting/electrical company)*

Tom runs across the stage and off the other side.

	What was that? *(Gems shuffle)* What are all these strange noises? Will you help me everyone? Will you call out if you see anything behind me? *(Tom runs across again. Aladdin turns just a moment too late)* Did you see something? Where? *(Repeat twice more. The third time Tom runs across, Aladdin turns in time to see him and they both scream)*
Aladdin	Who are you?
Tom	Tom
Aladdin	Tom?
Tom	Tom – the only flying carpet with mat nav!
Aladdin	A flying carpet! Can you fly me out of here?
Tom	I'm sorry – I can only fly round things, not through them.
Aladdin	Then I'll just have to think of something else. *(Looking through treasure)* Maybe there'll be something here that could help us. Hey! This would make a perfect ring for proposing to a beautiful princess!* *(Local jeweller)* ... If I ever get to see her again. *(Gems uncurl and stand up)* Hey! What's this? Who are you?
Gems	*(These lines could be divided up between the gems or spoken in unison)* We're gems that people love to own Because it makes them richer, But Aladdin you have wiser eyes – You see the bigger picture. We see in you a faithful heart, A love that's strong and true, So riches much more precious Are the ones we give to you.

Each does a twirl or bow/curtsey before speaking and handing Aladdin a gem.

Ruby Ruby, I bring a greater gift than wealth –
The ruby cheeks of glowing health!

Emerald I'm Emerald, green for growth you see,
Growth in loving kindness and integrity.

Goldie Gold am I, a sunny nature's what I bring!
More valuable than coins or pretty diamond rings.

Pearl I am Pearl, formed slowly in the oyster's shell,
I bring patience and a loyal heart as well.

Aladdin Thank you. You really are special gems! This is a truly magical place! We could do with a bit more light though. Let's see if this dirty old lamp would be any use. *(Rubs the lamp)*

SFX Genie CD Track 36

Genie jumps on stage followed by The Three Wishes, holding various certificates.

Aladdin Wow! Who are you?

Genie I'm the Genie of the Lamp and these are The Three Wishes, three yesses in dresses.

Three Wishes Hi Aladdin!

Genie We're from the lamp that likes to say yes and **we** are here for **you**. That means, you say it, I'll okay it! You want it, you got it! But there is a limit, so don't rush in! Think before you wish. I can grant you three wishes and only three; it's the magic number to you from me!

Aladdin *(In a daze)* Three wishes? For me?

Genie That's right. But I hope you'll take a little advice; I've been doing this a long time.

Three Wishes A very long time! *(They hold up certificates)*

Genie Look at all these qualifications I have in wish-granting! And no matter what anyone says, the exams aren't getting any easier. Now, I can't tell you what to wish for, but I can say beware of the detail. I once had a wildlife fanatic who wished to be close enough to a lion to feel its breath on his cheek. Of course, he forgot to ask to be invisible and the last we heard of him…

Three Wishes …was the lion burping.

Aladdin Oh dear!

Genie Look, why don't you just sit here and we'll go over it in our own, unique style!

SONG 4 JUST THREE WISHES *(See p78 for lyrics)* CD Track 7/22
[Genie/The Three Wishes]

During this song, The Three Wishes act as backing singers and there is scope for some lively dancing and for a brass section to appear with cut-out instruments to add to the mix!

Aladdin I think I know my first wish! Shall I run it past you first?

Genie Good idea! What is it?

Aladdin Can I wish to take all this treasure back to my home… and Tom of course!

Genie Aladdin, your wish is my command! Hold on to your hats, everyone, we're going out of here, and fast!

SFX Genie CD Track 36

All exit.

END OF ACT ONE

If appropriate, use **ALADDIN REFRAIN BT** *(CD track 16) as a playout.*

ACT 2

Scene 7: VILLAGE REVAMPED

Servants bring on tray of more food for the Sultan. There are two new signs: 'To Wishy Washy Laundry' (SR) and 'To Brand New Village Hall' (SL). There is a DJ positioned at far side of stage. Villagers mingle on stage. Jasmine and Aladdin enter SR.

ALADDIN REFRAIN 4 *(See p74 for lyrics)*   CD Track 8/23

DJ   Good morning *(local place)*. Here on Love Struck Radio, I'm Mr Right and I'm sending out 'lurve' vibes. I've got a request here from Al to his beautiful Jasmine – 'Will you say yes and make me 'Aladdin Heaven'?' Cheesy, but sweet. I hope it's a nod for you, Al!

Aladdin and Jasmine mime proposal and Jasmine nods.   Cue Card: Hooray!

Jasmine and Aladdin exit. Villagers remain, chatting happily in groups.

Scheherazade   *(Indicating Sultan who is clapping and giving thumbs up)*
The Sultan seems pleased – I hope you are too
Now our hero's found a love sweet and true!
But all can't run smooth – **that** I must mention!
Time for a twist, some dram-a-tic tension.
I must keep the plot line moving along
If I don't want this to become my 'swan song'!
So rocky's the road before Al can wed –
It's not that I'm mean, I'm just fond of my head!
Here comes our baddy now **with** a new plan –
To **come** by the **lamp**, he'll **do** all he **can**!

Abanazar enters at side of stage, disguised as an old pedlar.   Cue Card: BOO! HISS!

Abanazar   Silent, you stinky hairs in a monkey's armpit! I'll get back at these peasants! I **will** build my resort and knock down their pathetic village hall! I have a plan which is trickier than a SATS Level 6 algebra question! I will be Master of the Universe yet! You are watching a genius at work!   Cue Card: BOO! HISS!

New lamps for old! Think Ikea – out with the old, in with the new!

SONG 5   NEW LAMPS FOR OLD *(See p79 for lyrics)*   CD Track 9/24

During song, some villagers start to follow Abanazar, quite entranced, rather like children following the Pied Piper. They summon others and the crowd grows gradually as the music builds.

At end of song, Abanazar mimes transacting with a couple of villagers. Matt Paint and Wal Paper enter, driving a cardboard van, signwritten: 'Matt Paint and Wal Paper, Superior Decorators, watching paint dry since 1990'.

Matt   OK, that's the village hall all finished. What's next, Wal?

Wal   Aladdin's house, Matt. We're to decorate the Granny annex for Widow Twankey. She wants it to be sleek and modern but with a few distressed pieces.

Matt   That sounds like Mr/s _____ from the local school, Wal.

Wal   *(Indicating box)* This must be the stuff they want chucking out.

Matt   Carefully recycling, you mean.

Wal   Naturally, Matt. *(Picking up lamp)* I don't think you could recycle this old thing though, definitely past its sell-by date.

Matt   Bit like Widow Twankey!

Abanazar   New lamps for old! New lamps for old!

Villager   What's that? Sounds almost too good to be true!

Wal	Here, old man, Wal Paper at your service. *(He offers the lamp)* How about swapping this for a new one? I'll take it home to Mrs Paper.
Matt	**Lou** will like that Wal. *(Pause. To audience)* Lou... Paper. Oh, please yourselves!
Abanazar	Certainly sir. Just give it to me and you can take your pick.

As soon as Abanazar has the lamp, he throws off his disguise and holds it up triumphantly.

Abanazar	At last! I have unlimited power!
Matt	Are you with Sky?
Abanazar	Quiet, you hairy knee of a flea! A little rub and the world will be at my command!

SFX Genie CD Track 36

Genie jumps on stage.

Genie	Yo! Aladdin... oh, it's you!
Abanazar	Yes, it's me! And I command you to make me the most powerful man in the east!
Genie	*(Very miserably)* Your wish is my command.

SFX Genie *(Abanazar responds with a little shimmy)* CD Track 36

Abanazar	Ooh, now I feel just like *(headteacher/chair of governors)*. Come with me, we have plans to put into action. **Cue Card: HISS! BOO!**

All exit.

Scene 8: LAUNDERETTE INTERIOR

Enter Widow T 'carried' on rickshaw by Mr Rick and Mr Shaw (on the back is hung a sign: 'Heavy load on board').

Widow T	Hello everyone! I'm so happy. My boy marrying into royalty – I feel just like Carole Middleton! What an exciting day! And I've just had a lovely ride in this new invention. They can't think what to call it, but it's marvellous!
	Bye Mr Rick! Bye Mr Shaw!
Rick/Shaw	Bye Gorgeous. *(Both wink at her and exit)*
Widow T	I've got an interview later with Washer Woman's Weekly! Can you believe they want to slap me... on the front cover of their next edition?! And shoot me... on video in my beautiful launderette. Oh! Here's my brand-new machine arriving!

Salesman enters with machine.

Salesman	Cleans like a dream, incredibly green, hardly costs a bean, look at that sheen! Sign here on the dots, no more mucky spots! *(He exits)*
Widow T	Wishy, Washy! Come and see this! *(They enter)*
Wishy	Okey
Washy	Dokey!
Widow T	I can see it all now, we'll be just like 'Glossy Goss' magazine. All the celebs will bring their dirty laundry to us!

SONG 6   WISHY WASHY LAUN-D-RY *(See p80 for lyrics)* CD Track 10/26

This song lends itself to some visual humour. There could be children dressed as boxes of soap powder blowing bubbles and some dressed as a line of washing, side-stepping across the stage. There could also be some items which go 'into' the machine dirty and 'come out' sparkling.

Widow T	Come on you two, we'd better smarten up, we're going up in the world!
Wishy	Hoity!
Washy	Toity! *(All exit.)*

Scene 9: THE VILLAGE

Aladdin and Jasmine enter.

Aladdin I'm so happy, Jasmine. You're like a bus to *(local place)*.

Jasmine What?

Aladdin I feel like I've waited all my life for you!

Jasmine Well, I think you're like a net full of haddock!

Aladdin Eh?

Jasmine A really good catch!

Aladdin Together we're like *(local team)* v. *(local team)*.

Jasmine Football teams?

Aladdin The potential for a really good match! Now that the new village hall is ready, all we have to do is perfect our double act!

Enter Widow T.

Aladdin Hi Mum! Hey, have you seen the old lamp that was in my house? I can't find it anywhere!

Enter Abanazar, a couple of guards, Wantu and Genie.

Abanazar That's because it's not yours anymore, 'Aladdin trouble!' *(To guards)* Hold him! *(Grabbing Jasmine)* And neither is she! I think I might marry her myself.

Jasmine I'll never marry you, you venomous viper!

Abanazar We'll see about that, my little firebrand. If you don't, I may have to throw your father and all his useless collections into the deep, dark ocean. *(To villager)* Call the police!

Villager The Police!

Enter the police in two-by-two formation, running, bringing their knees as high as possible and making 'Nee-naw' sound. They should not speak until they arrive on stage.

Police We seek 'em here, we seek 'em there,
We seek those crim'nals everywhere.
No stone unturned, we can't be tricked,
We grab 'em and we say 'You're nicked!'

PC Bright PC Bright and PC Crook at your service.

Abanazar PC Crook? That's not a very good name for a policewoman!

PC Crook It is when your first name's **Katya**! *(Winks at audience)*　　　Cue Card: Groan!
Oh, please yourselves!

Abanazar Take Aladdin and throw him into the most rat-infested jail. Lock Princess Jasmine in the Palace with her father. You can plan the wedding of the year, my dear!　　Cue Card: BOO! HISS!
(To audience) And don't think you'll get off lightly! I'll make you watch repeats of *(current really annoying TV programme)*.

The police take Al & Jasmine off in different directions.

Aladdin Jasmine!

Jasmine Aladdin!

Wantu Troublesome toads, he's not just the baddy!
Now he's taken the lamp, **he's** the **daddy**!

Abanazar *(To Wantu)* And you can go and find someone else to annoy, you slimy rhymer. I can afford a professional now, like *(Alastair Campbell)*. Go on, shoo!　　Cue Card: Ahh!

All exit.

ALADDIN REFRAIN 5 *(See p74 for lyrics)*   CD Track 11/26

Aladdin and Jasmine enter and stand on separate sides of the stage gazing outwards.

Scene 10: PRISON/PALACE

Aladdin   Oh Jasmine, just when everything…

Jasmine   …seemed to be turning out right…

Aladdin   …and now it's all…

Jasmine   …going wrong!

Aladdin   I really thought we…

Jasmine   …were meant to be together for ever.

SONG 7   **I STILL BELIEVE** *(See p81 for lyrics)*   CD Track 12/27
[Jasmine/Aladdin]

At end of song a couple of rats scurry across the stage, then re-enter. During the following section, when Aladdin is speaking, Jasmine and the King freeze, and vice versa.

Aladdin   I never thought I'd envy a rat, but at least you can come and go as you please! Hey, I've got an idea! Can you get me some paper? *(They nod and do it. Aladdin scribbles on the paper)* Please take this message to my mum, Widow Twankey.

(Rats look worried) No don't look scared, she's not as bad as she looks. Oh Jasmine, there may be hope yet! *(Freezes)*

Rats walk across the stage, looking at note.

Rat 1   What's it say?

Rat 2   Mum, get Tom…

Rat 1   Tom?

Rat 2   …Tom to fly you, Wishy and Washy into the Palace, then you can distract Abanazar while they get the lamp back and try to bring it to me. Love 'Aladdin jail'.

Rat 1   He's still got a sense of humour then. *(Exit)*

Aladdin remains frozen. Jasmine paces up and down, then suddenly stops, having had an idea.

Jasmine   Father, don't you have a collection of hankies used by famous people? How many have you got?

King   Oh, lots! They come up quite often on eBay. **'S-not** expensive!

Jasmine   And you've still got a collection of old keys that might come in useful one day?

King   Yes.

Jasmine   Then I've got a plan! Let's knot the hankies together and climb out of the window. We'll take the keys and hopefully find one that will open Aladdin's cell. *(Both look knowingly at audience)* Come on, let's get knotting! *(All exit, including Aladdin)*

SCENE 11: THE PALACE

Abanazar enters and places the lamp upstage. Widow T could have a selection of undies and tights to show Abanazar.

Widow T   Knock, knock!

Abanazar   Who's there?

Widow T   Boo.

Abanazar   Boo who?

Widow T	*(Entering)* There's no need to cry, I've come to help you out!
Abanazar	I don't need any help.
Widow T	*(Guiding him to front of stage, as Wishy and Washy sneak in)* Even a Master of the Universe has to have clean undies! I'll get your whites so white, you'll glow in the dark! I'll fit you out with some Widow Twankey fancy pantsys! The slicker knicker! *(Shows him some undies)* If you're going to be wearing them over your tights like a real superhero, they have to be something special!
Abanazar	Hmm. I'd like to have my very own slogan embroidered on them…
Widow T	Of course. How about LOL?
Abanazar	LOL? What's that?
Widow T	Lord of the Lamp of course.

Wishy and Washy get the lamp and sneak out. Widow T spots this.

Widow T	*(Exiting quickly)* Anyway, you just think it over. I must go and hoover me bloomers.
Abanazar	What? LOL? Hmm. *(Spots that the lamp has gone, then shouts)* The lamp! Stop thief! Guards, after her! *(Runs off)*

Scene 12: THE VILLAGE

Enter Aladdin, Jasmine and King, running on.

Aladdin	I think we've given the police the slip!
Jasmine	I'm so glad one of your keys fitted the jail cell, father! I'll never complain about your collections again. *(All look knowingly at audience as before)*
King	That's good, Jasmine, because I've just started collecting odd socks.
Aladdin	You should have a word with my mum! Let's see if we can find her! *(Exit)*

SONG 8   **THE CHASE** *(See p82 for lyrics)*   CD Track 13/28

Aladdin catches the lamp and rubs it.

SFX Genie   CD Track 36

Genie appears.

Genie	Hey! Aladdin! It's good to have you back. I didn't like having Abanazar for a master.
Aladdin	Well, Genie, you'll never have to worry about that again! From now on, you'll be your own master. I wish to set you free! *Cue Card: Hooray!*
Genie	Oh Aladdin, that's great! I'll go and tell the girls. But I won't be leaving town right away, you might need a good wedding singer! *(He exits)*
Aladdin	But we haven't had time to sort out a wedding.
Widow T	I used to watch *Blue Peter*, here's one I arranged earlier!

Mr Rick and Mr Shaw enter, with the rickshaw now decorated as a bridal car.

Jasmine	What more could we ask? We've got true love, *Cue Card: Ahh!* great friends and the perfect place for our reception – the new village hall! *Cue Card: Hooray!*
Widow T	Come on you two lovebirds. Let's get you to the church on time!

Jasmine and Aladdin get in rickshaw and exit, followed by Widow T, Wishy, Washy and King. Villagers remain, chatting in groups.

Villager 12	Three cheers for Aladdin and Jasmine! Hip, hip, hooray! *(Etc.)*

Genie re-enters carrying the lamp:

Genie	Hey everyone! I'm free!	*Cue Card: Hooray!*
	It's better than that!	*Cue Card: Hooray!*
	(Handing the lamp to audience member) Take this and give it a rub!	
	(In 'pre-recorded' voice) I'm sorry, there's nobody home right now, the Genie of the Lamp is free!	*Cue Card: Hooray!*
	You're really getting the hang of that now!	

          I'm so proud of Aladdin, setting me free when he could have wished for anything at all, even *(local issue)*. What a great friend! And do you know what? I've always longed to be a rock and roll guitarist but I couldn't make my own dreams come true. But look what the girls have given me as a leaving present. An air guitar! And a fab sound effect!

SFX Guitar Hero Riff   *CD Track 37*

          You see, sometimes it just takes thoughtful friends and a bit of imagination to make your dreams a reality!

Scene 13: CHURCH EXTERIOR

MC   Would you all please rise!

SONG 9   WEDDING PROCESSION *(See p84 for lyrics)*   CD Track 14/29

During song, villagers form an arc facing the audience. Towards the end of the song they split off evenly to either side of the stage, leaving a gap for Aladdin and Jasmine, who process off through the audience.

Widow T	*(Wiping a tear)* Oh that was so lovely.
Wishy	Lovey.
Washy	Dovey.
King	*(To Widow T)* I hear we have an interest in odd socks in common. Why don't you come to dinner and we'll see what we can pair off.
Widow T	*(Aside, winking at audience)* I can think of one odd pair right away!

Police enter with Abanazar, possibly in overalls.   *Cue Card: BOO! HISS!*

PC Bright	This fellow is going to do community service. Meet the new caretaker of the village hall! And here's your supervisor. *(Enter Wantu)*
Wantu	I'm glad to say the table's turned, I hope a lesson you have learned!

Aladdin and Jasmine re-enter on stage if possible (or else back through the audience).

Genie	Hey Aladdin, don't forget you've still got one wish left!	
Aladdin	Then I wish we could do a production like this every year!	
Scheherazade	The Sultan enjoyed the tale so much That my head and neck can stay in touch!	*Cue Card: Hooray!!*
	But tonight a new tale he'll expect – I'll sort out later what to do next! So clap your hands and stamp your feet, And even get up from your seat, To cheer the gifted cast and crew Who performed this panto just for you!	

SONG 10   A PANTO LIKE NO OTHER! *(See p85 for lyrics)*   CD Track 15/30

This song provides the perfect opportunity to take a bow and say thank you to all your helpers! (A condensed, faster version is also on the CD (track 38) to allow the cast to exit the stage.)

THE END

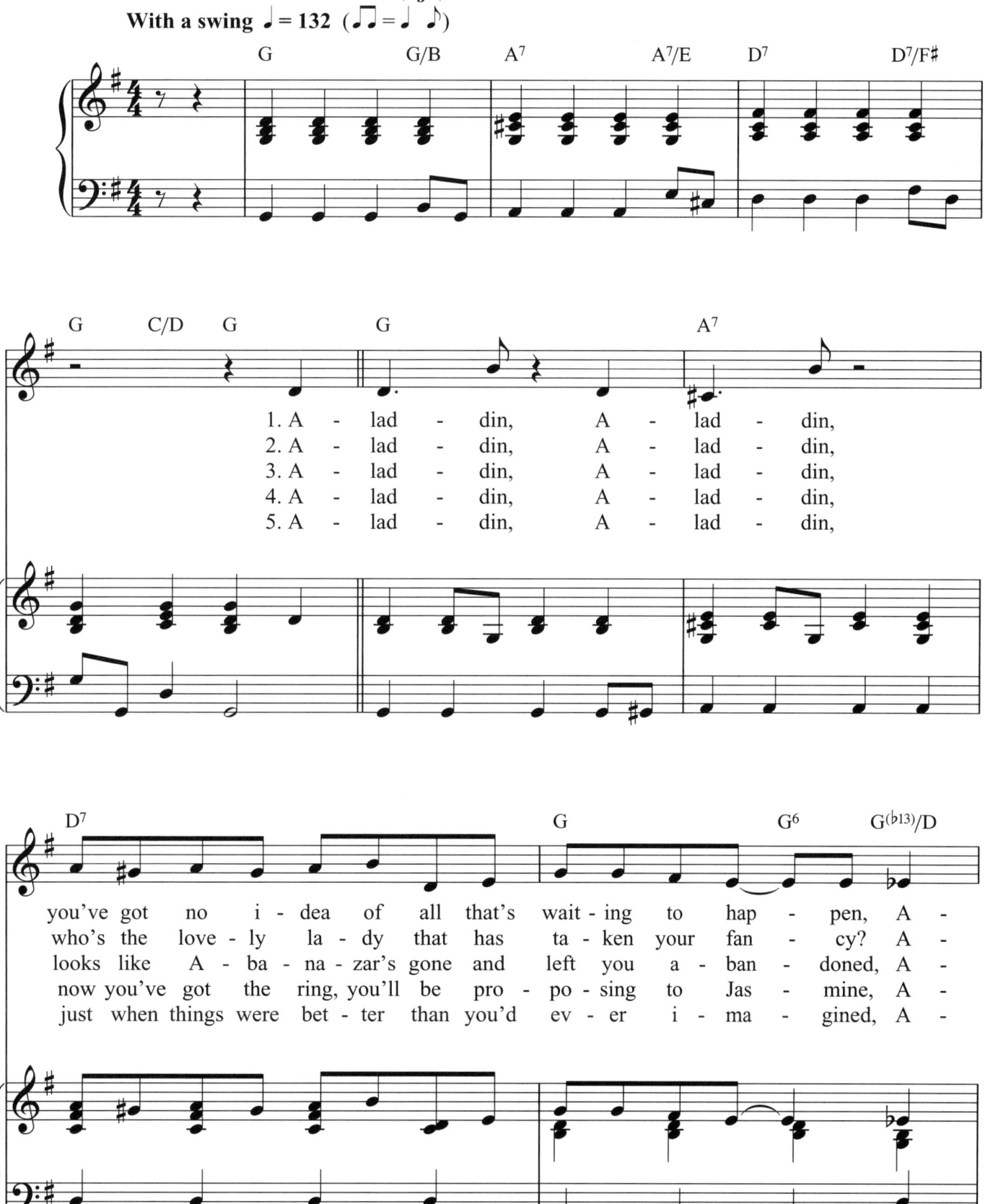

In The Marketplace

Villager 4: I'll have ten metres for my wife!
Wife: Oi! Don't be cheeky, you distant cousin of a gnat!

Words and Music by
Mark and Helen Johnson

© 2014 Out of the Ark Ltd, Middlesex TW12 2HD
CCLI Song No. 7004525

I've Had Enough

Maid 1: Don't be too keen to give up being royal, being ordinary's not all that!

Words and Music by
Mark and Helen Johnson

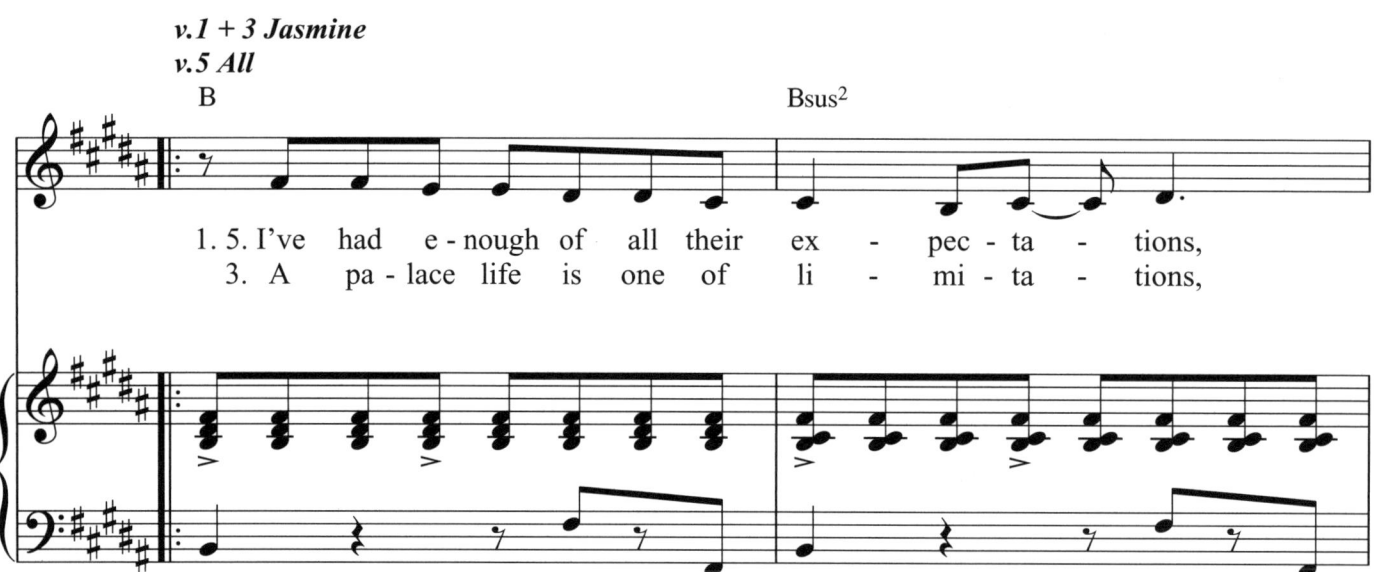

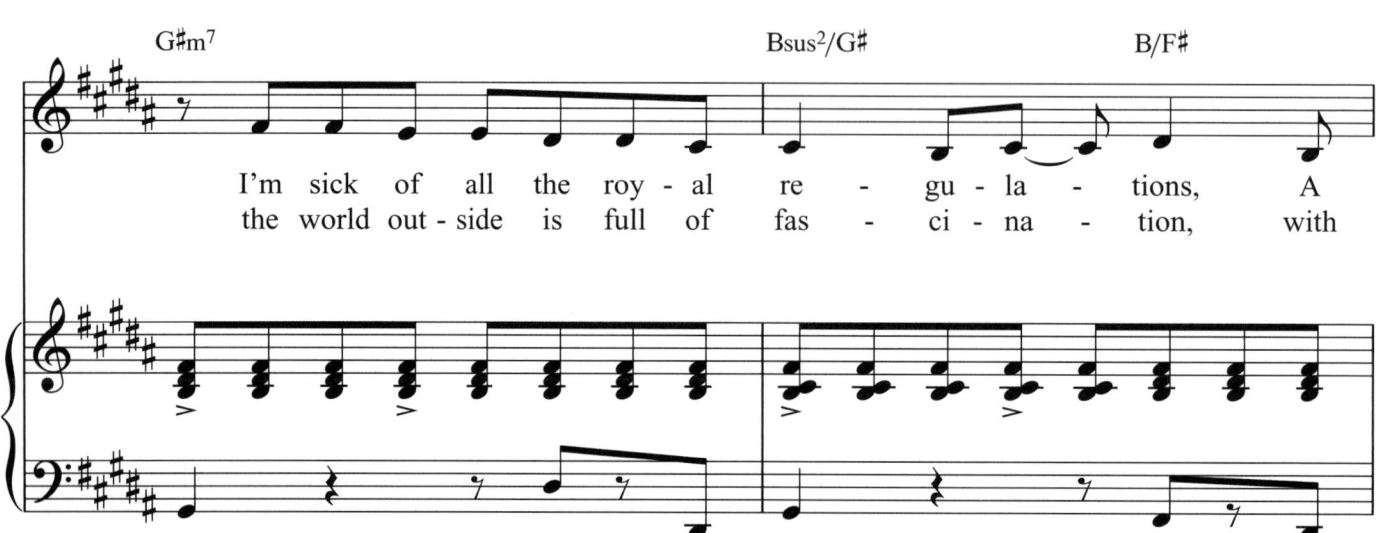

© 2014 Out of the Ark Ltd, Middlesex TW12 2HD
CCLI Song No. 7004523

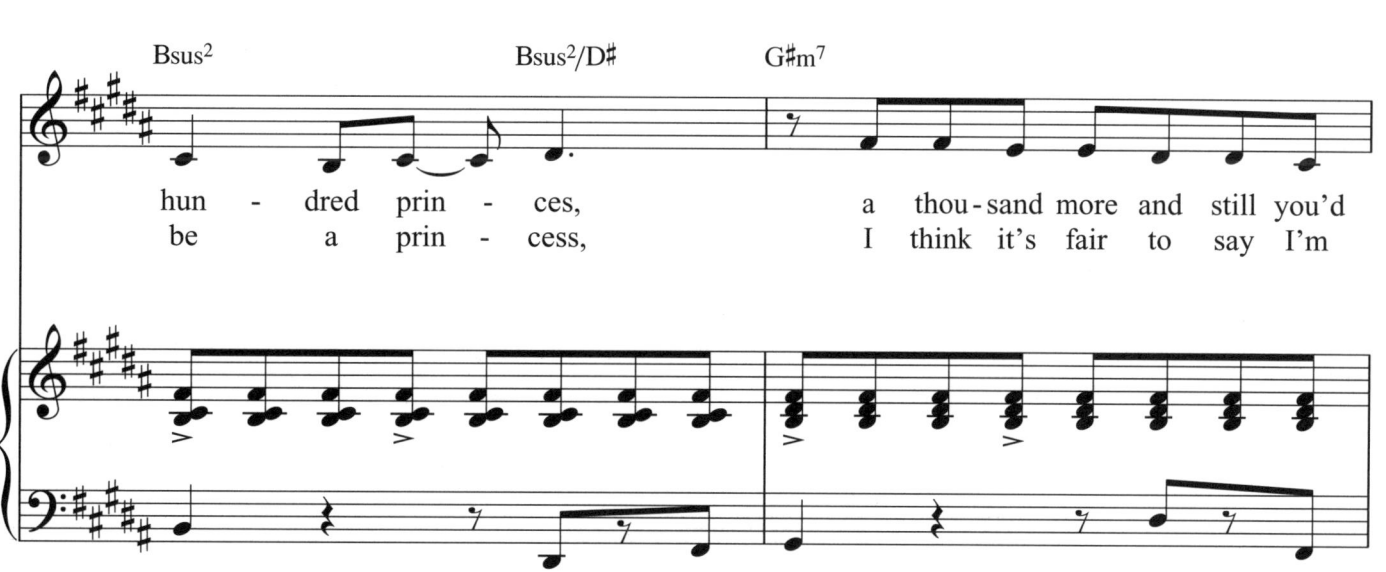

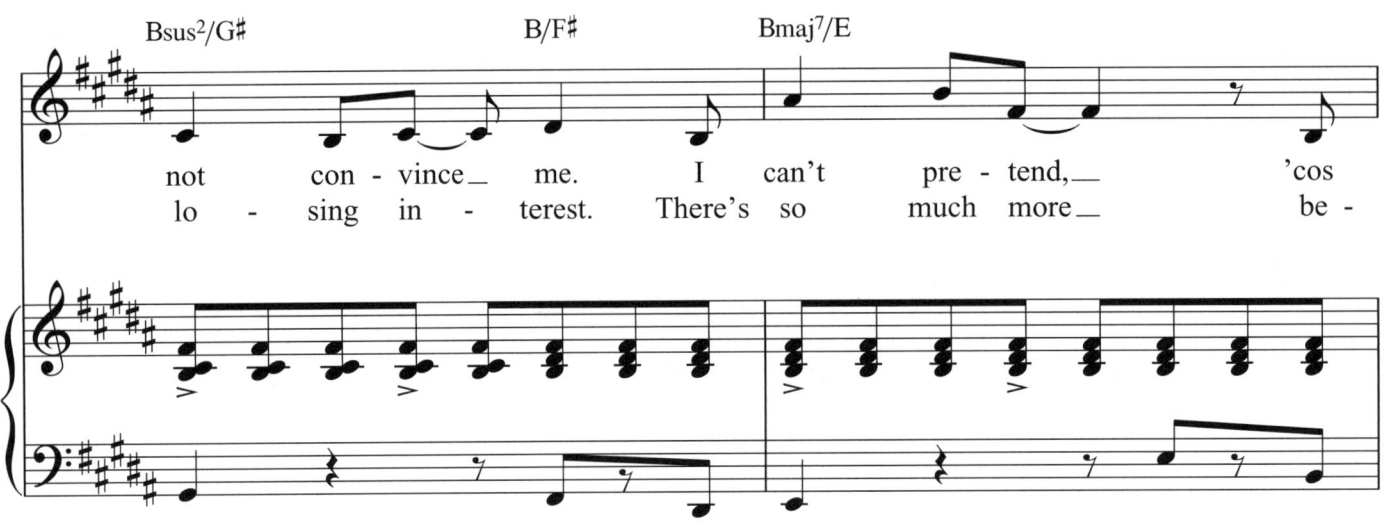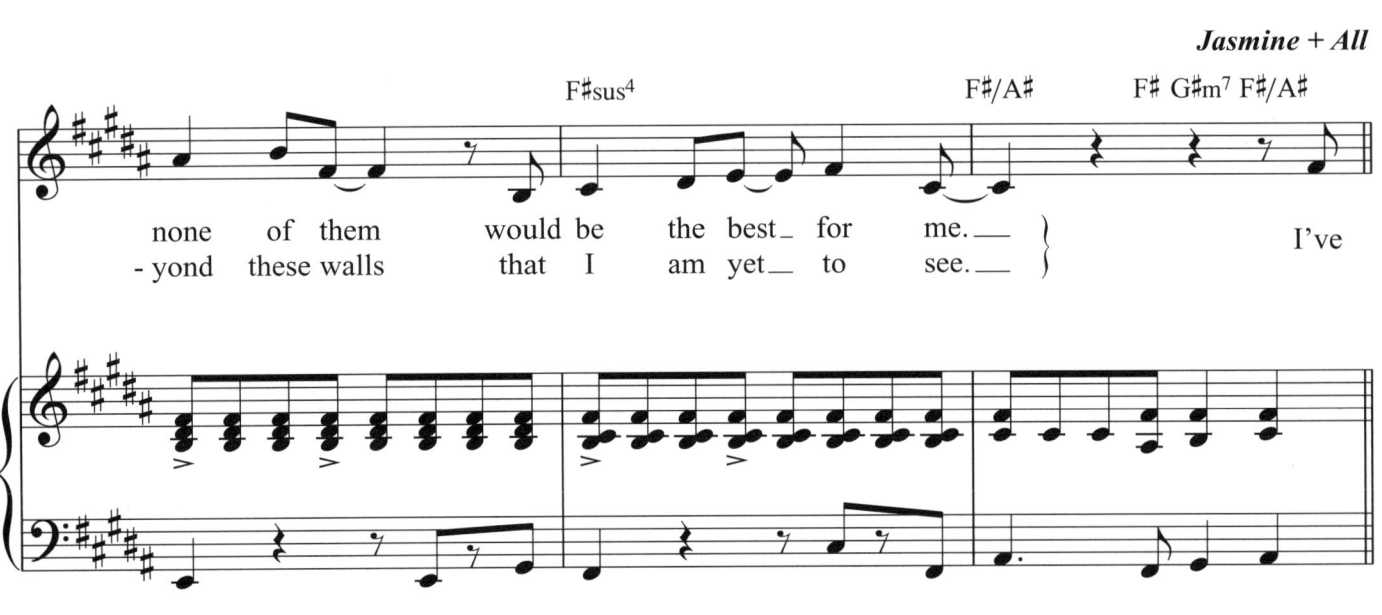

Some Things Go Together Perfectly

Jasmine: A tickled onion!
Aladdin: Hey, we could be a double act!

Words and Music by
Mark and Helen Johnson

© 2014 Out of the Ark Ltd, Middlesex TW12 2HD
CCLI Song No. 7004529

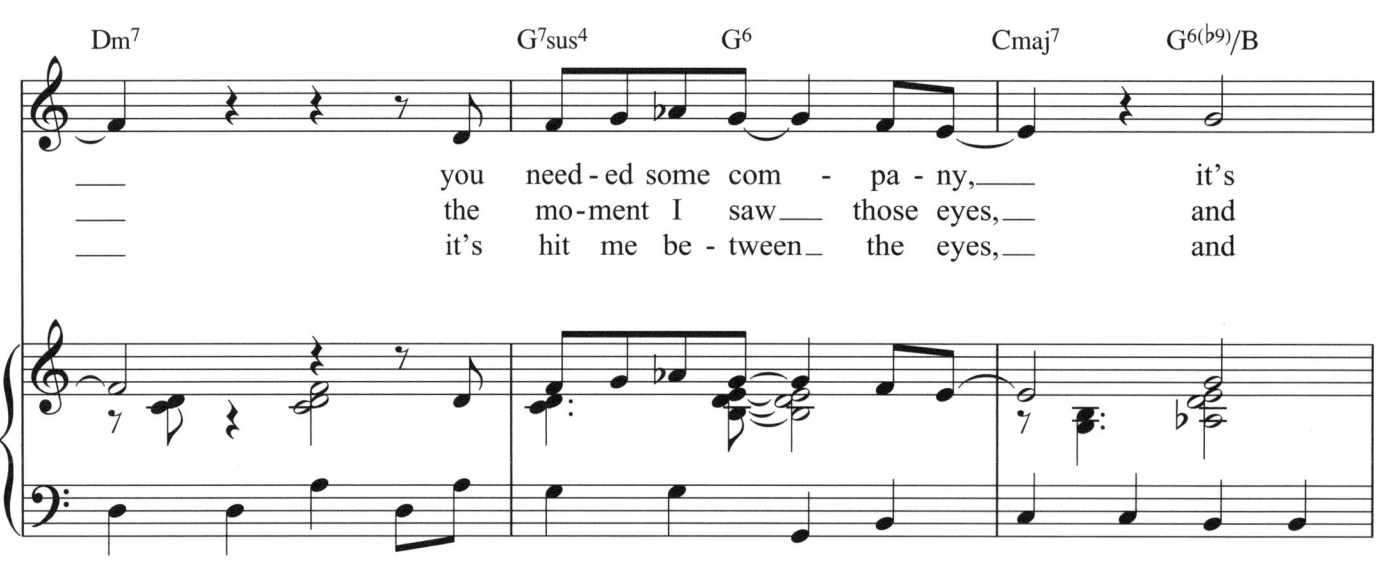

Just Three Wishes

Genie: Look, why don't you just sit here and we'll go over it in our own, unique style!

Words and Music by
Mark and Helen Johnson

© 2014 Out of the Ark Ltd, Middlesex TW12 2HD
CCLI Song No. 7004537

v.1 Genie
v.2 Genie + The Three Wishes
All sing on repeat

1. 3. Ev - ery - thing you've al - ways want - ed, a - ny - thing you ask,
2. 4. I could make you rich and fa - mous, e - lo - quent and wise,

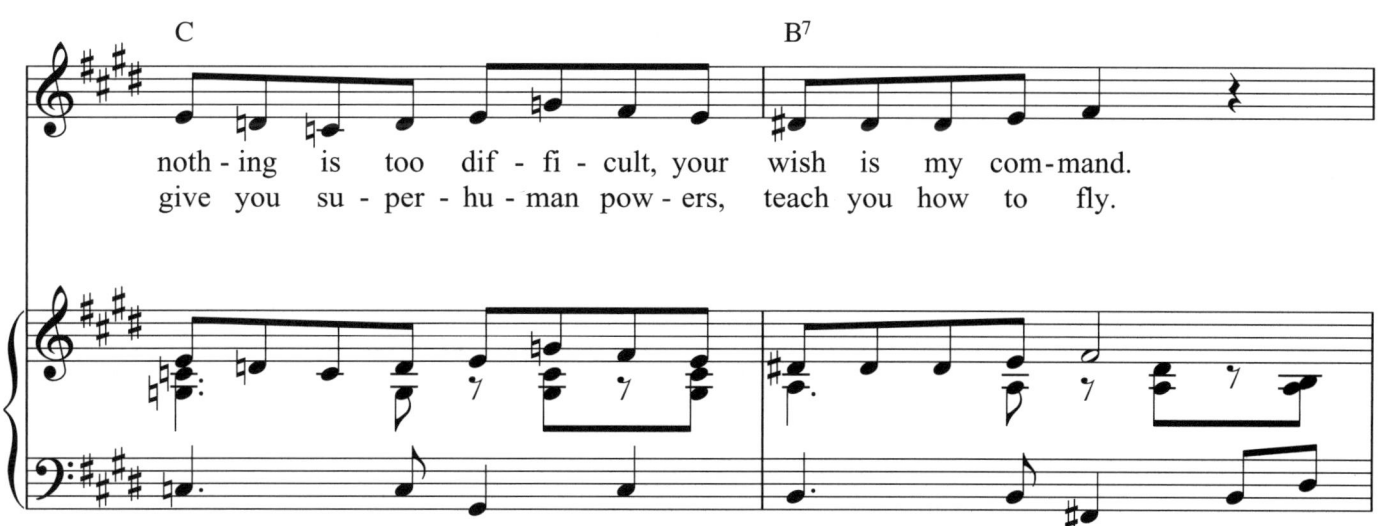

noth - ing is too dif - fi - cult, your wish is my com - mand.
give you su - per - hu - man pow - ers, teach you how to fly.

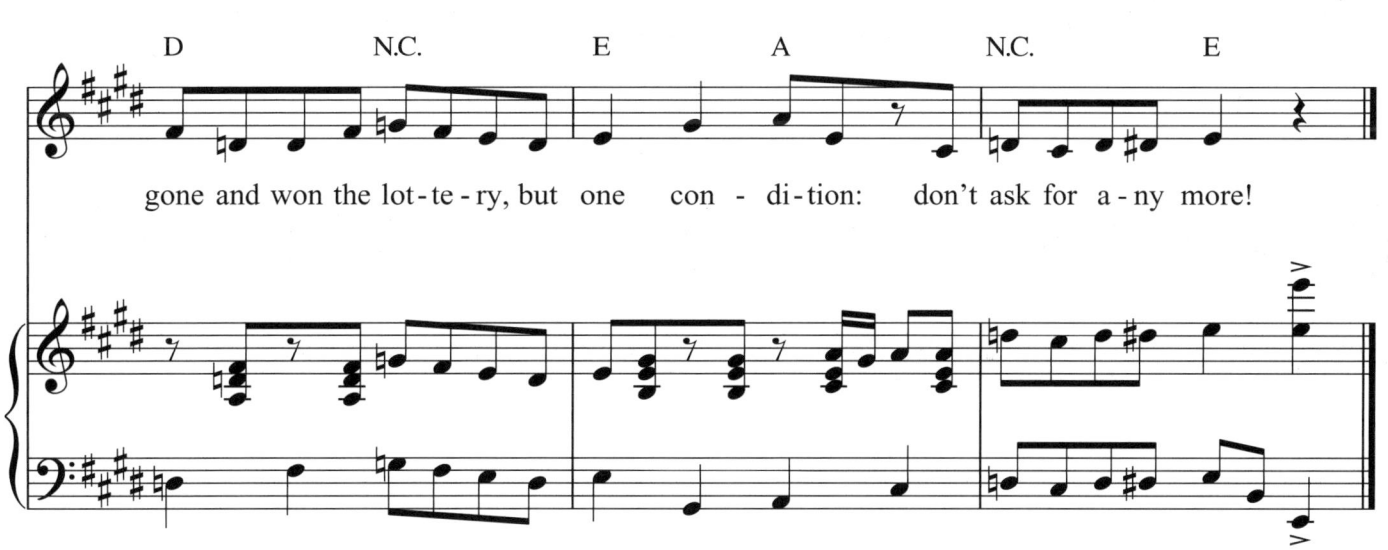

New Lamps For Old

Abanazar: New lamps for old! Think Ikea – out with the old, in with the new!

Words and Music by
Mark and Helen Johnson

1. New lamps for old!

New lamps for old! Bring me your rub-bish, I'll turn it to gold!

© 2014 Out of the Ark Ltd, Middlesex TW12 2HD
CCLI Song No. 7004526

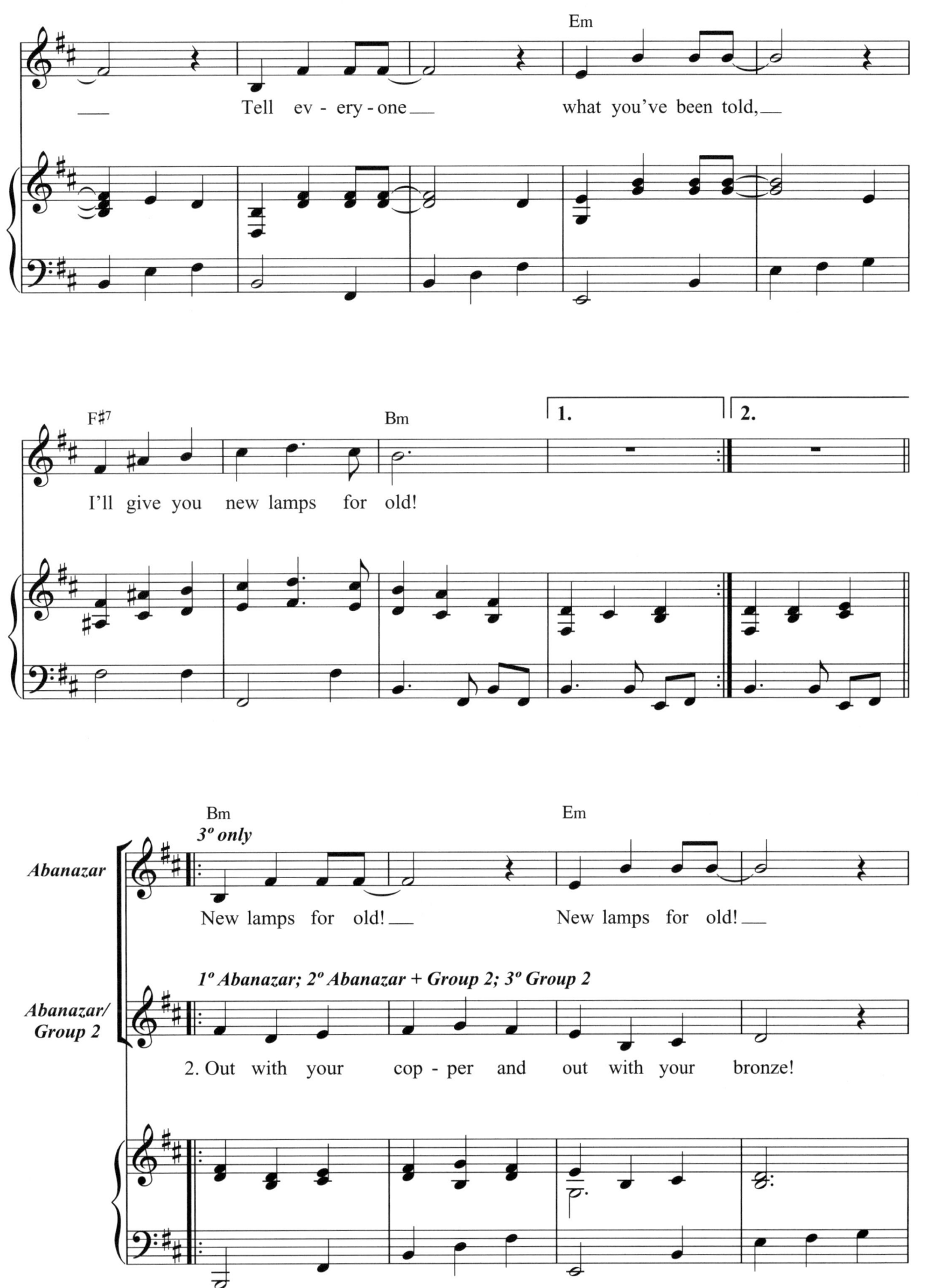

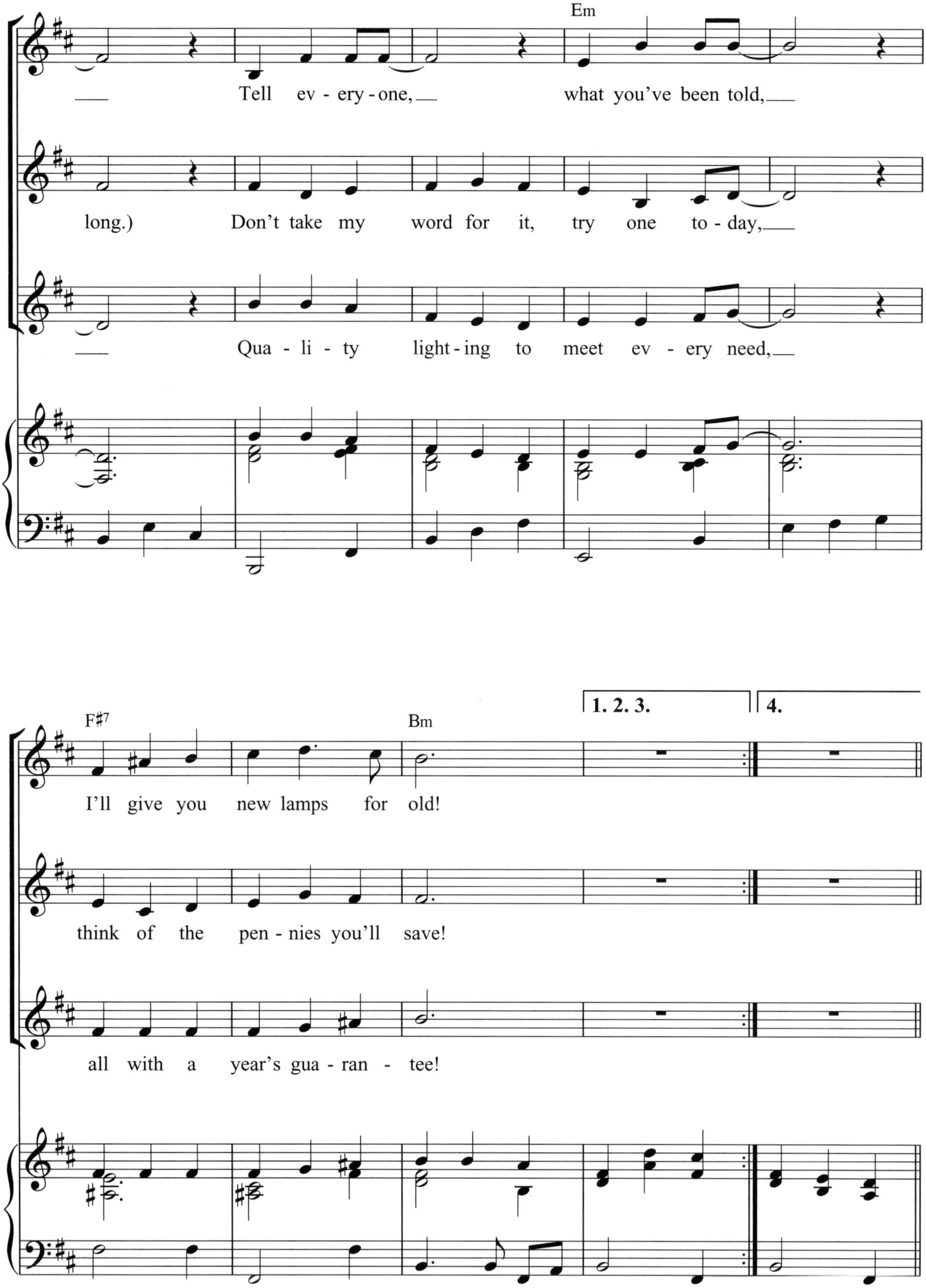

Tell ev-ery-one, what you've been told,
long.) Don't take my word for it, try one to-day,
Qua-li-ty light-ing to meet ev-ery need,

1. 2. 3. | **4.**

I'll give you new lamps for old!
think of the pen-nies you'll save!
all with a year's gua-ran-tee!

Wishy Washy Laun-d-ry

Widow T: I can see it all now, we'll be just like 'Glossy Goss' magazine. All the celebs will bring their dirty laundry to us!

Words and Music by
Mark and Helen Johnson

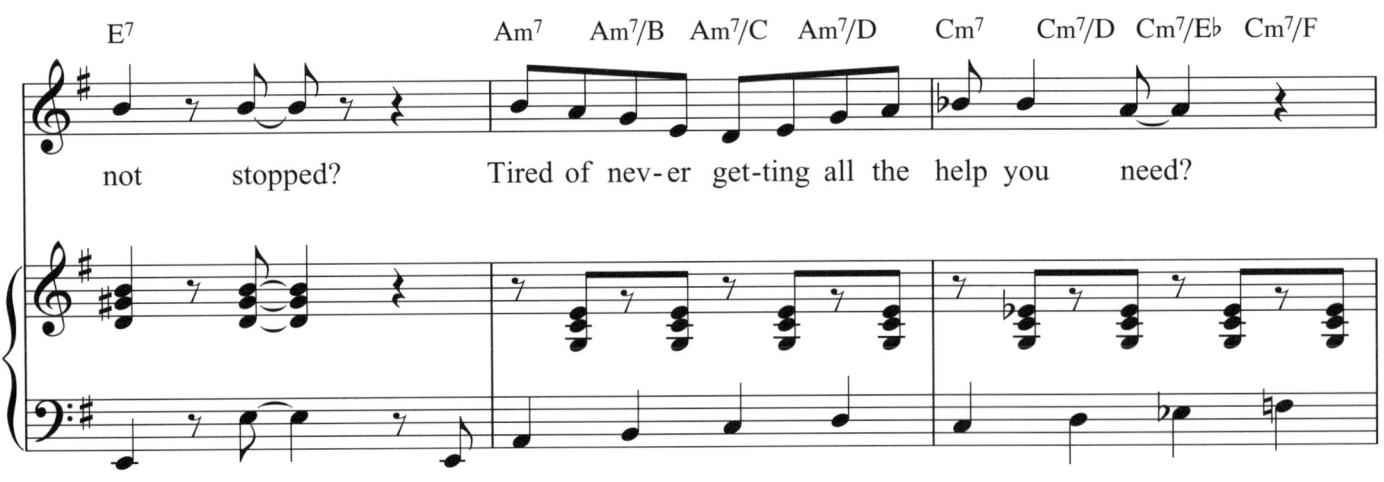

© 2014 Out of the Ark Ltd, Middlesex TW12 2HD
CCLI Song No. 7004536

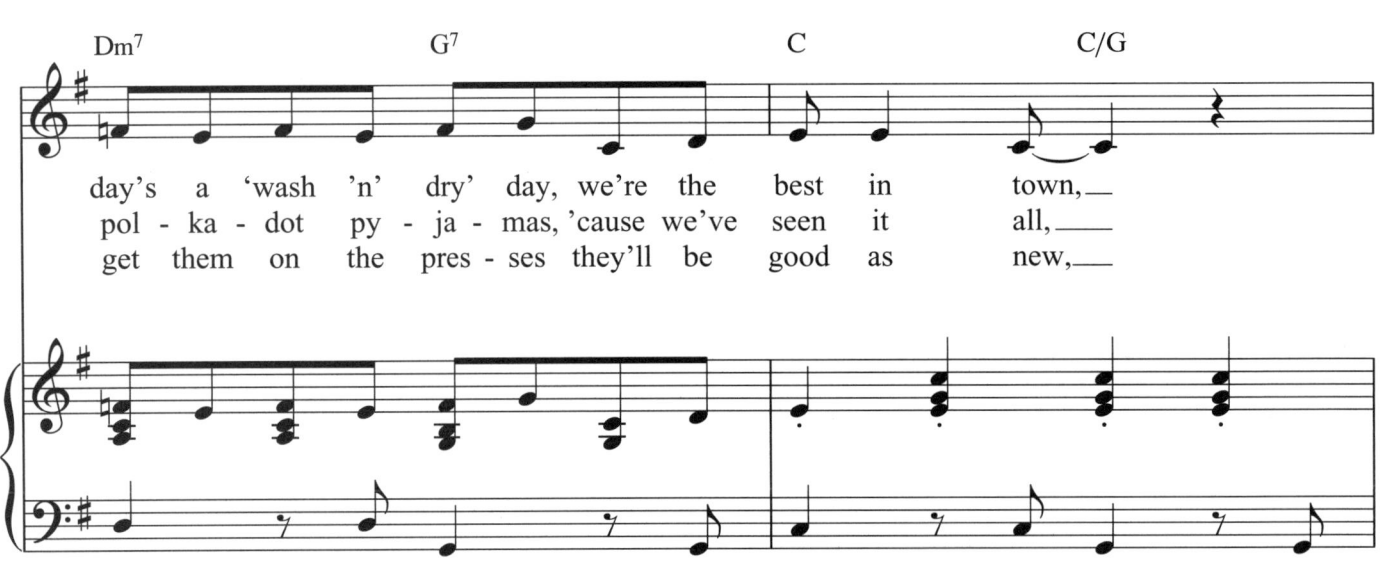

I Still Believe

Aladdin: I really thought we...
Jasmine: ...were meant to be together for ever.

Words and Music by
Mark and Helen Johnson

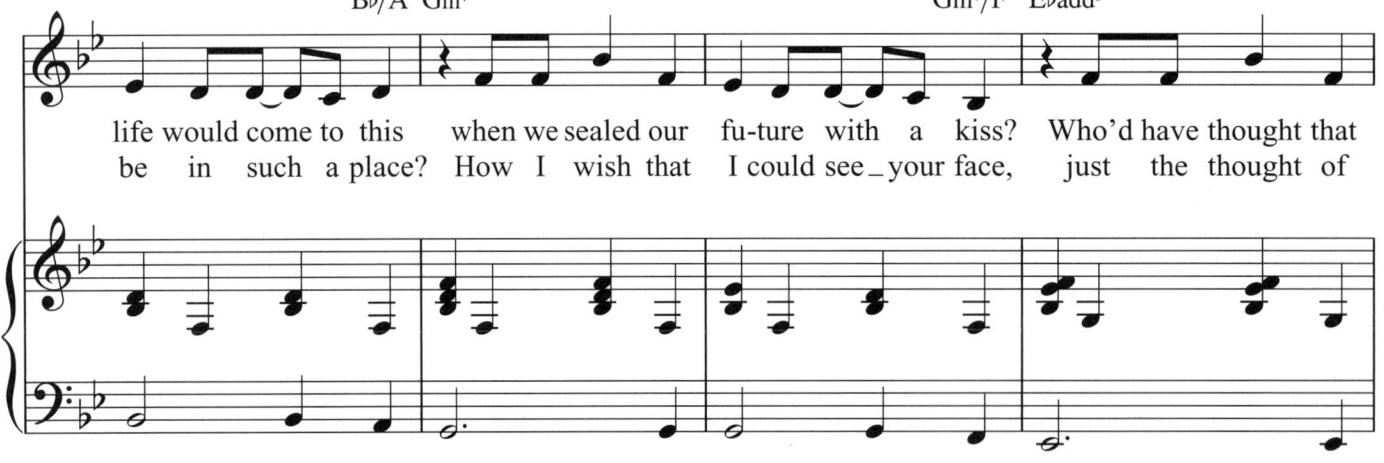

life would come to this when we sealed our fu-ture with a kiss? Who'd have thought that
be in such a place? How I wish that I could see your face, just the thought of

ev-ery-thing could change so pain-ful-ly? *Aladdin* From the day we
lo-sing you is tear-ing me a-part. *Aladdin + Boys* If I thought there's

© 2014 Out of the Ark Ltd, Middlesex TW12 2HD
CCLI Song No. 7004520

The Chase

Aladdin: You should have a word with my mum! Let's see if we can find her!

Words by Mark and Helen Johnson
Music based on a theme from
Peer Gynt Suite No. 1 by Edvard Grieg,
adapted by Mark and Helen Johnson

Gradually getting faster ♩ = 92-170

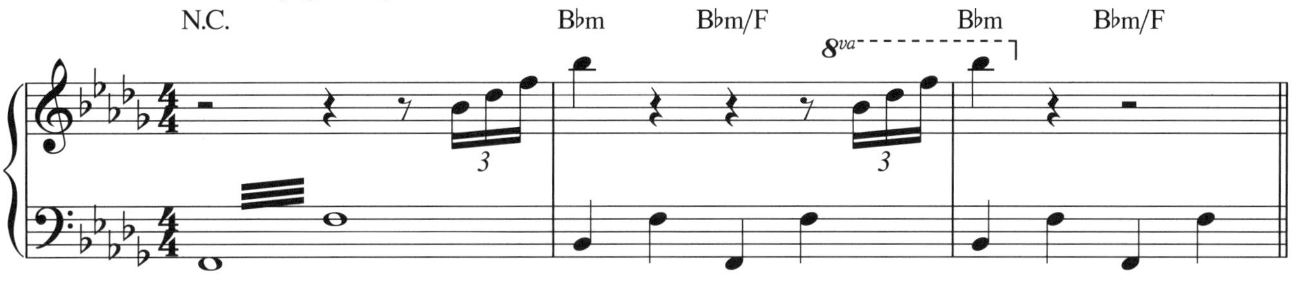

Group 1: Widow Twankey, Wishy, Washy
Group 2: Abanazar + 2 Guards
Group 3: Aladdin, Jasmine, King

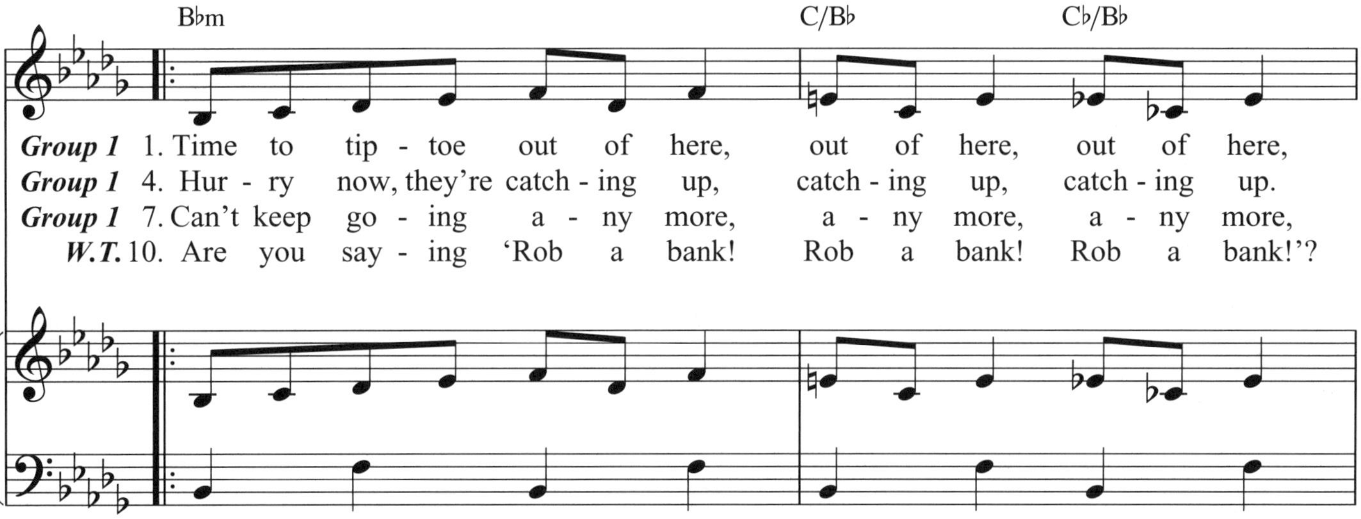

Group 1 1. Time to tip-toe out of here, out of here, out of here,
Group 1 4. Hur-ry now, they're catch-ing up, catch-ing up, catch-ing up.
Group 1 7. Can't keep go-ing a-ny more, a-ny more, a-ny more,
W.T. 10. Are you say-ing 'Rob a bank! Rob a bank! Rob a bank!'?

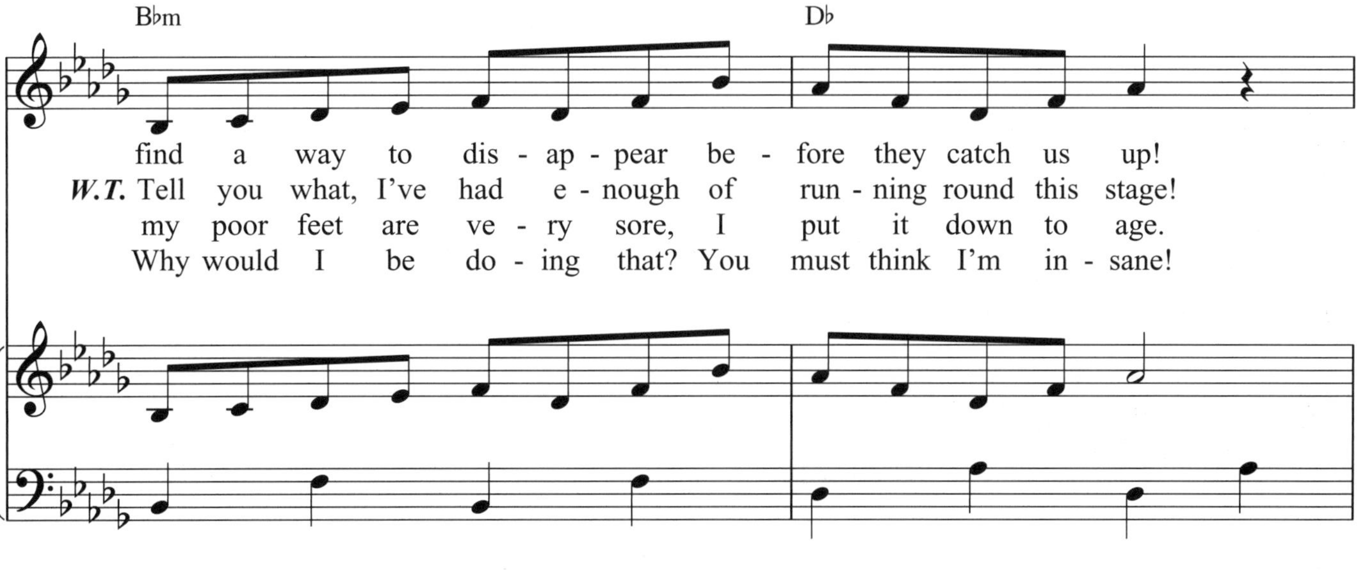

find a way to dis-ap-pear be-fore they catch us up!
W.T. Tell you what, I've had e-nough of run-ning round this stage!
my poor feet are ve-ry sore, I put it down to age.
Why would I be do-ing that? You must think I'm in-sane!

© 2014 Out of the Ark Ltd, Middlesex TW12 2HD
CCLI Song No. 7004532

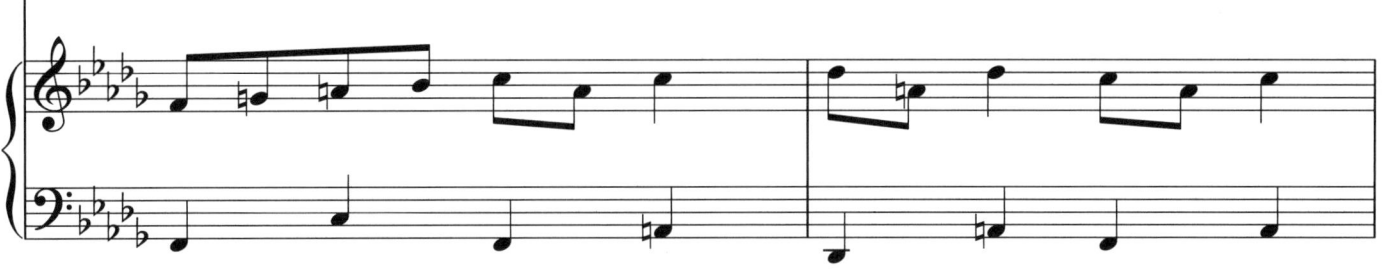

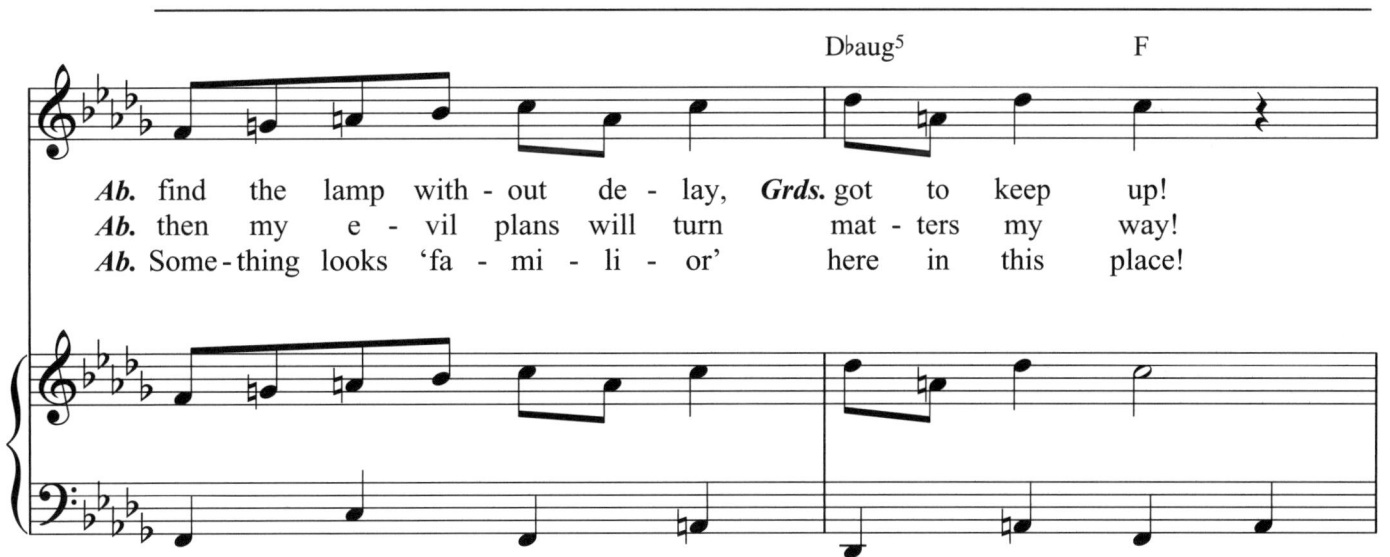

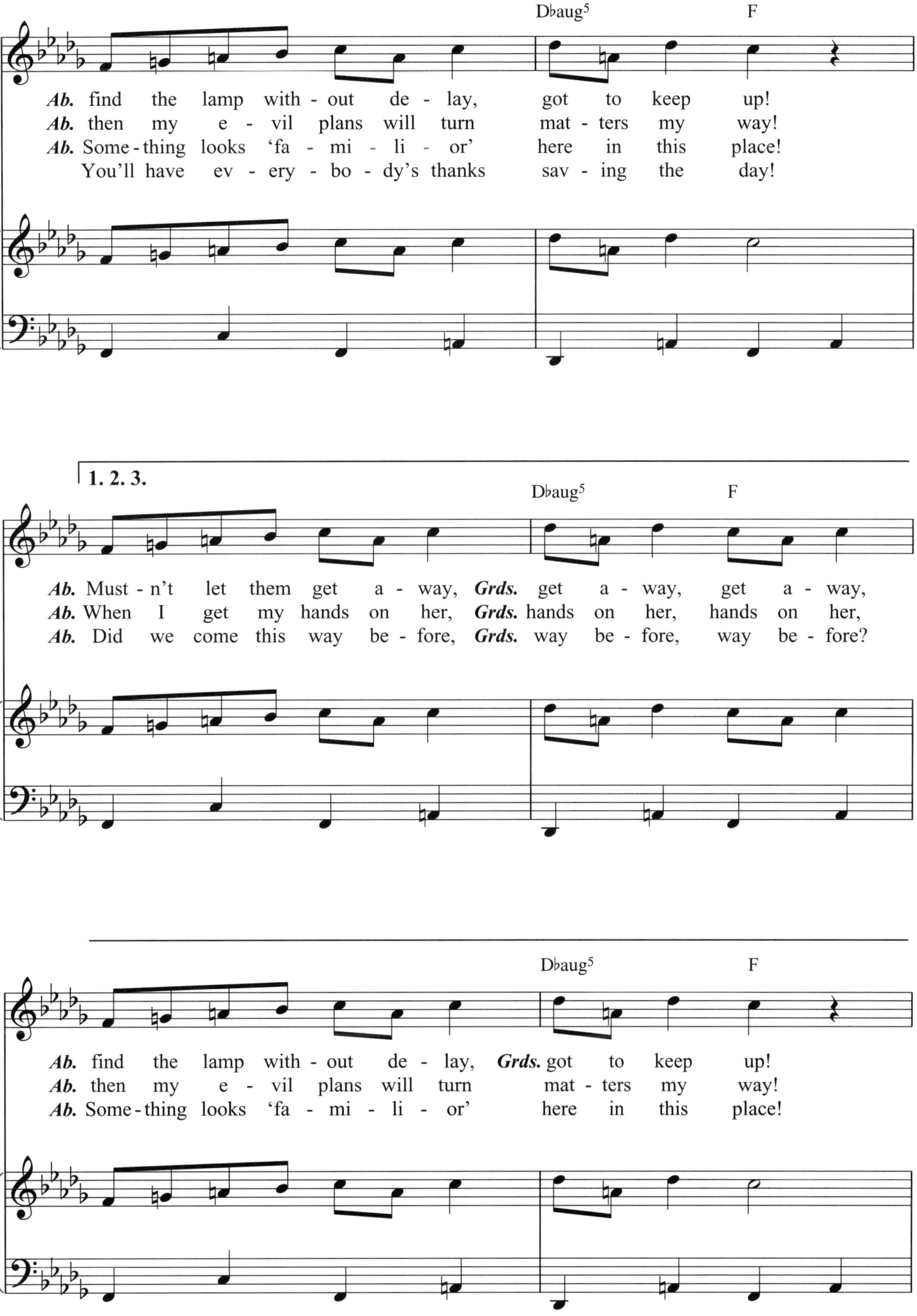
Db♭aug5
F
Ab. find the lamp with - out de - lay, got to keep up!
Ab. then my e - vil plans will turn mat - ters my way!
Ab. Some - thing looks 'fa - mi - li - or' here in this place!
You'll have ev - ery - bo - dy's thanks sav - ing the day!
1. 2. 3.
D♭aug5
F
Ab. Must - n't let them get a - way, Grds. get a - way, get a - way,
Ab. When I get my hands on her, Grds. hands on her, hands on her,
Ab. Did we come this way be - fore, Grds. way be - fore, way be - fore?
D♭aug5
F
Ab. find the lamp with - out de - lay, Grds. got to keep up!
Ab. then my e - vil plans will turn mat - ters my way!
Ab. Some - thing looks 'fa - mi - li - or' here in this place!

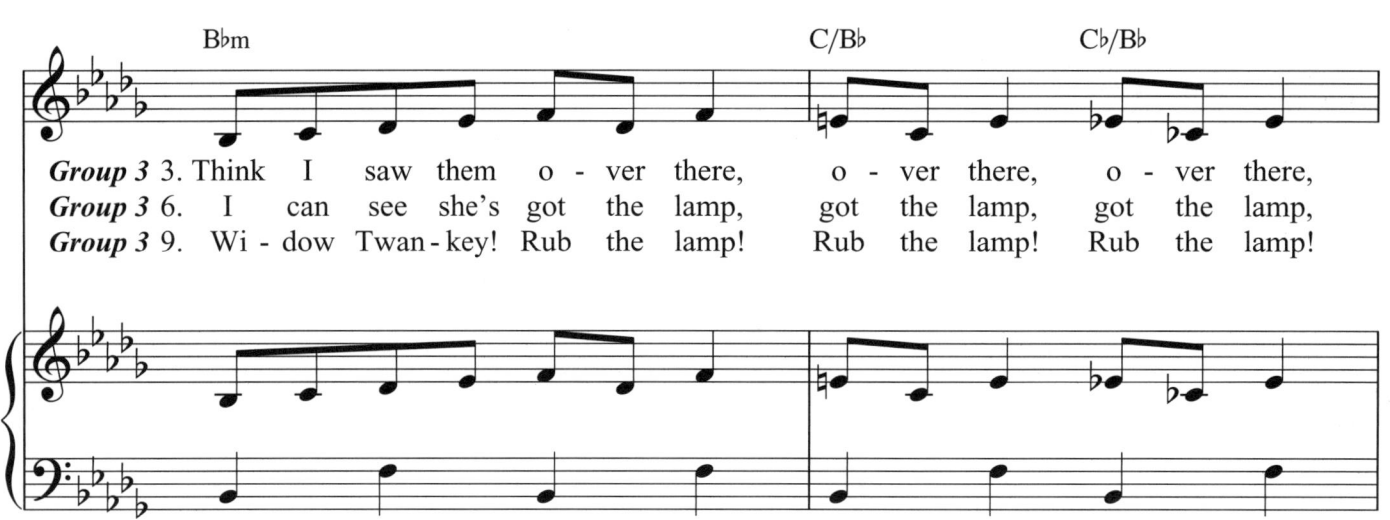
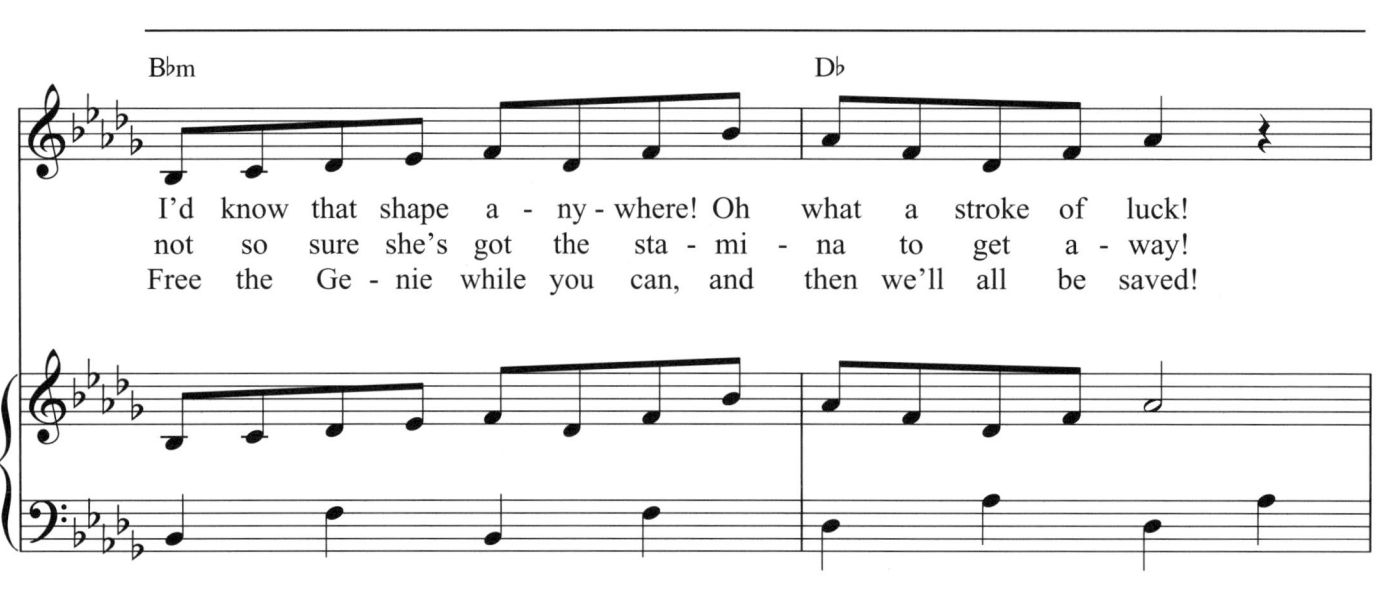
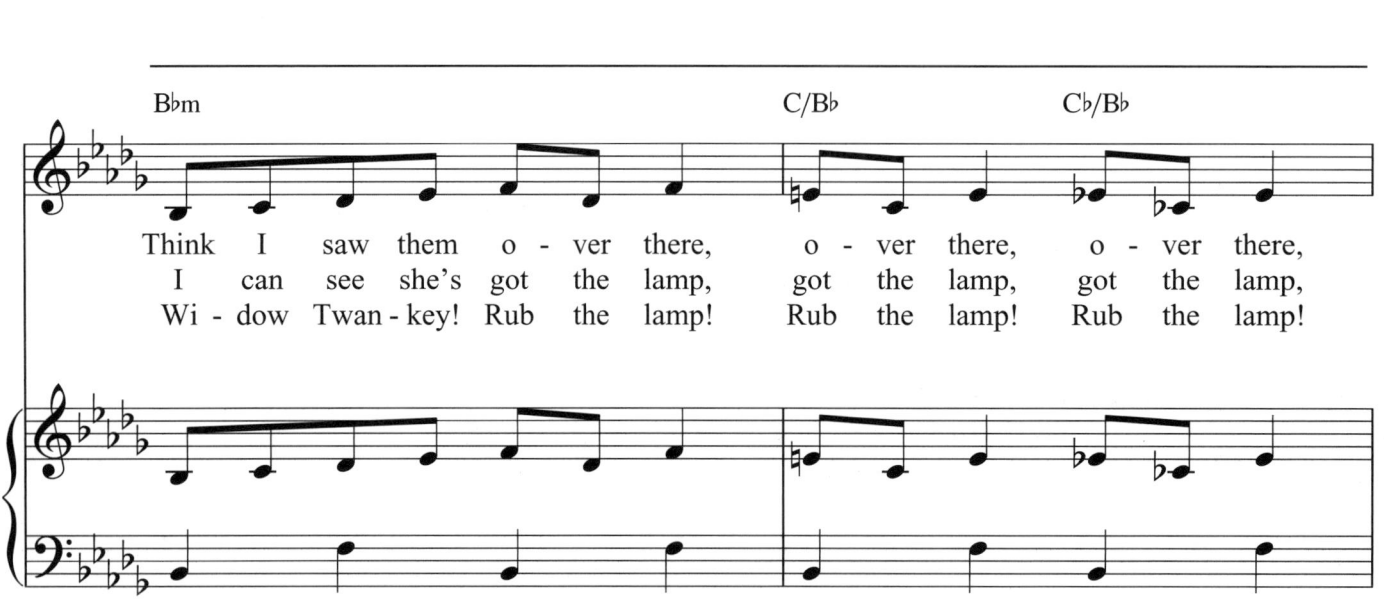

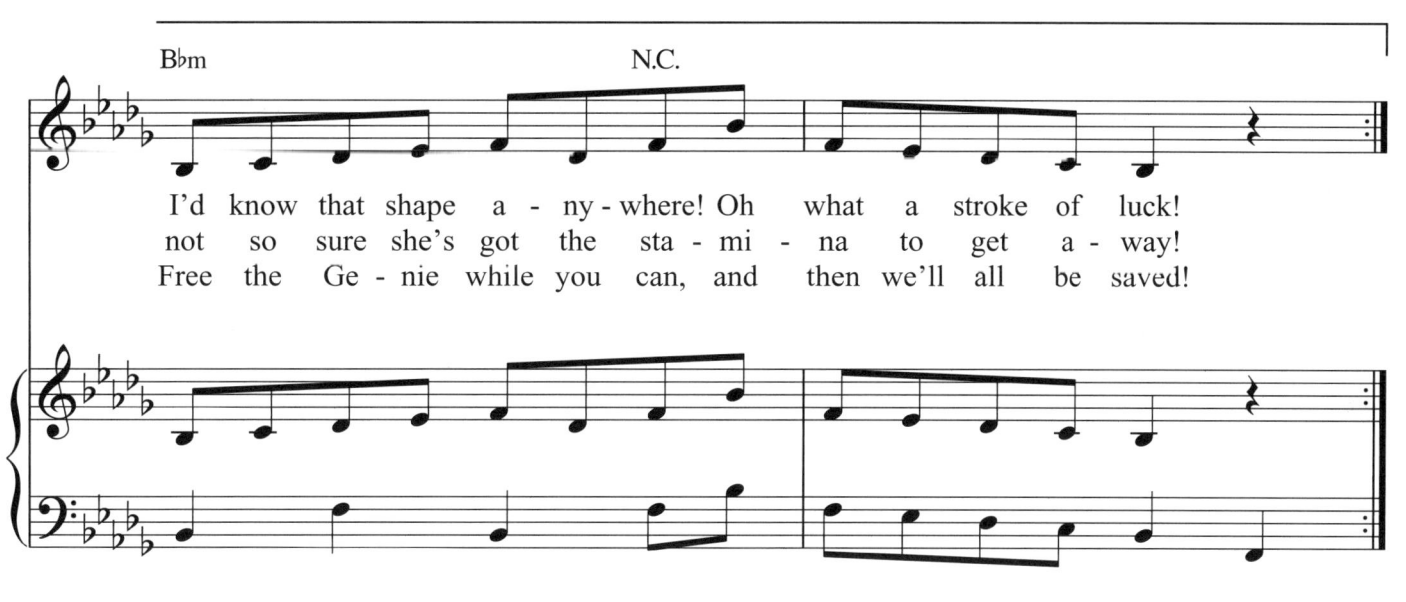
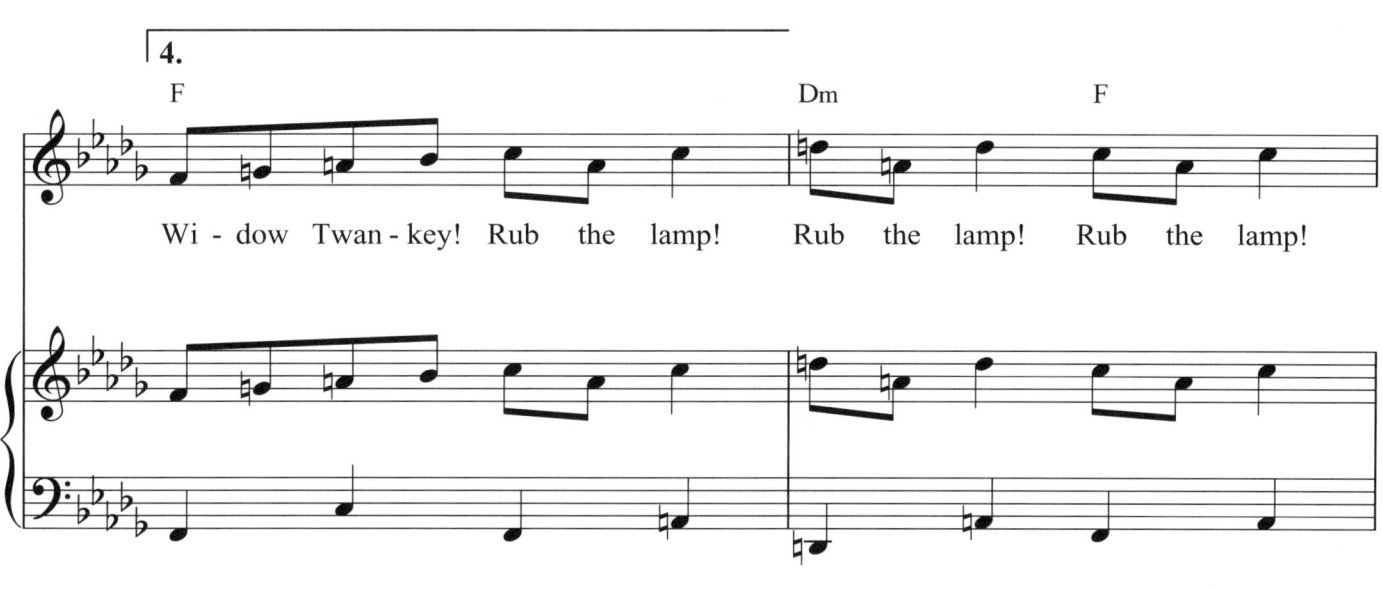
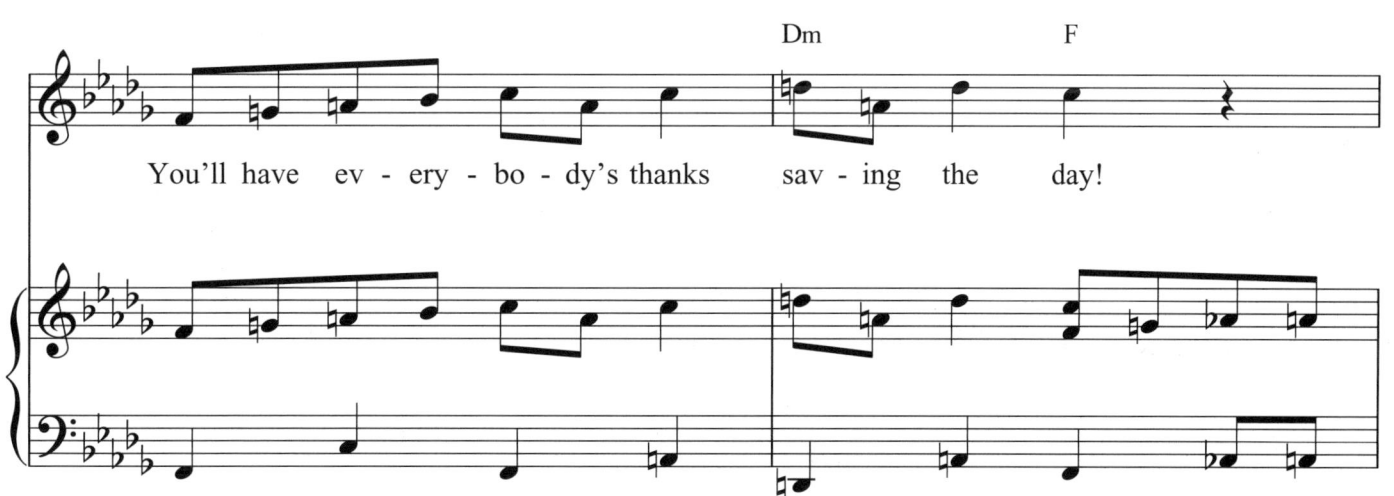

Wedding Procession

MC: Would you all please rise!

Words and Music by
Mark and Helen Johnson

Regal and gorgeous! ♩ = 72

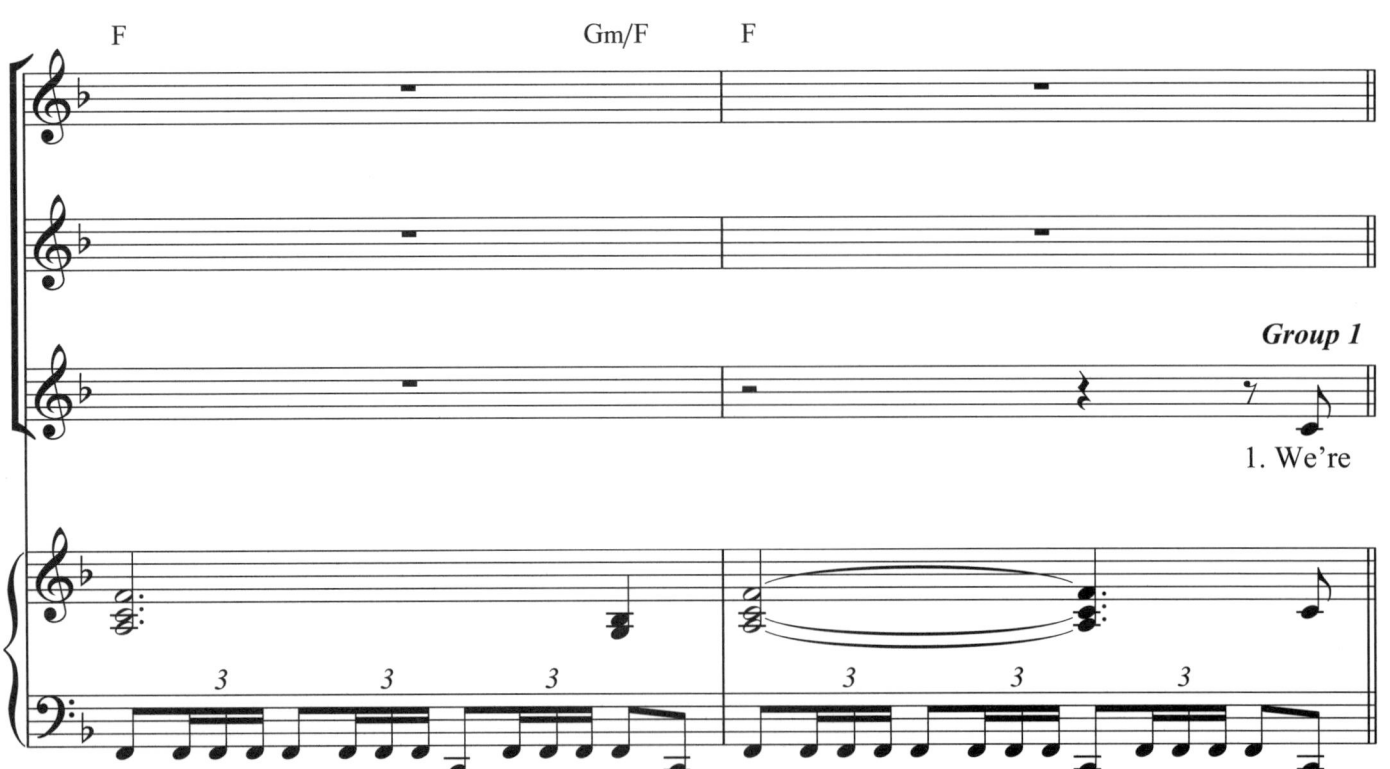

© 2014 Out of the Ark Ltd, Middlesex TW12 2HD
CCLI Song No. 7004535

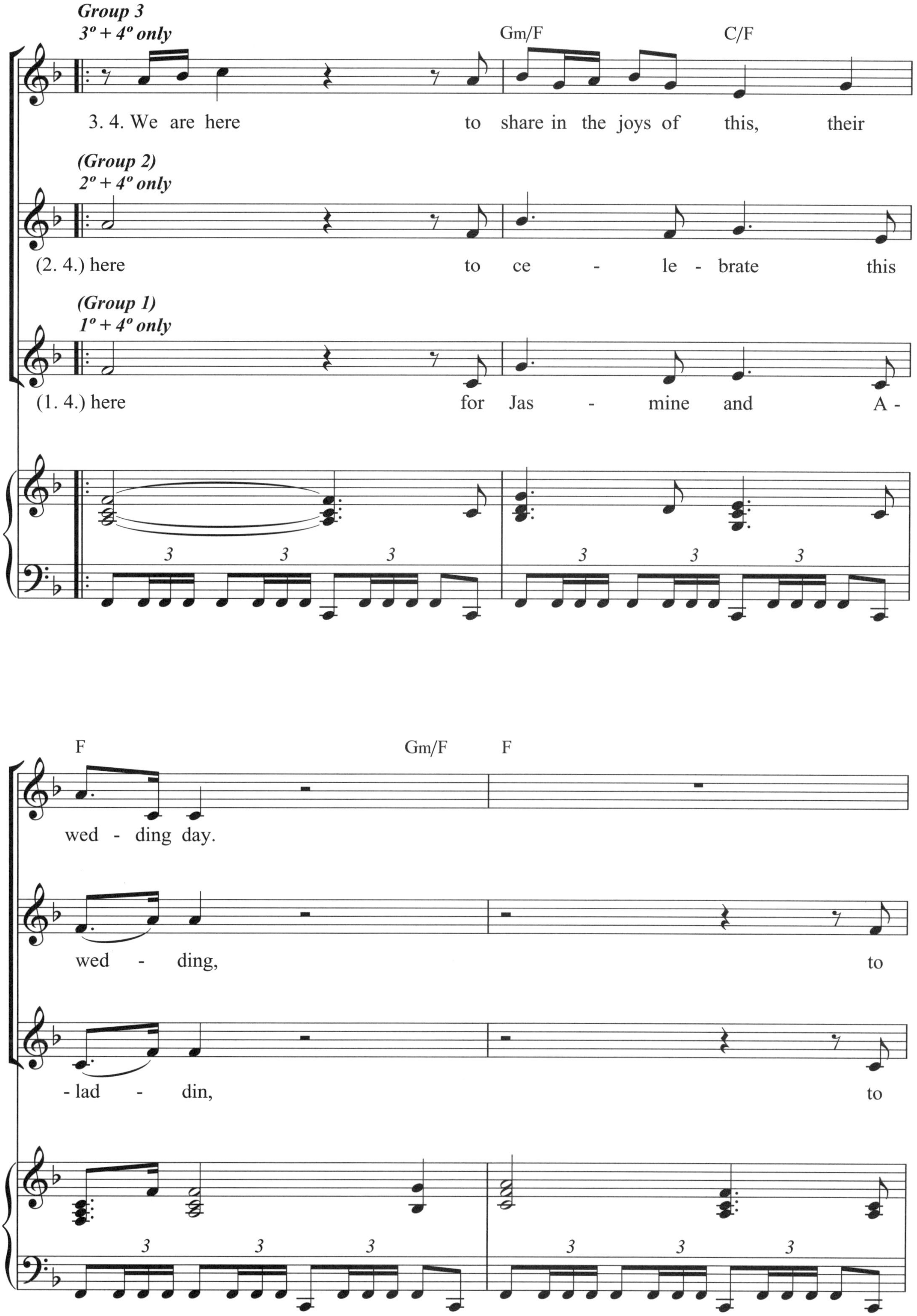
Group 3
3º + 4º only
Gm/F
C/F
3. 4. We are here to share in the joys of this, their
(Group 2)
2º + 4º only
(2. 4.) here to ce - le - brate this
(Group 1)
1º + 4º only
(1. 4.) here for Jas - mine and A -
F
Gm/F
F
wed - ding day.
wed - ding, to
- lad - din, to

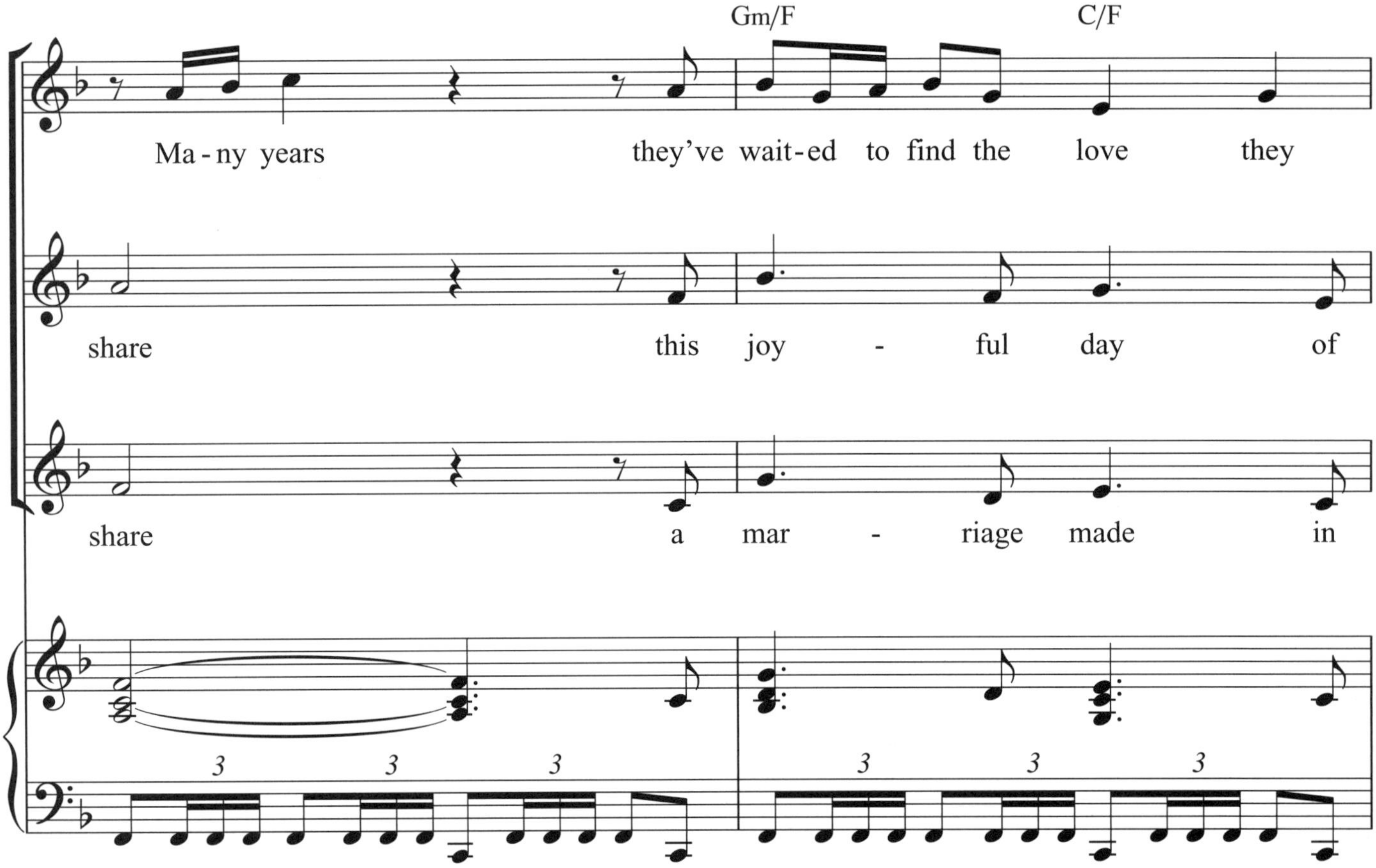
Gm/F
C/F
Ma - ny years they've wait - ed to find the love they
share this joy - ful day of
share a mar - riage made in
3 3 3 3 3 3

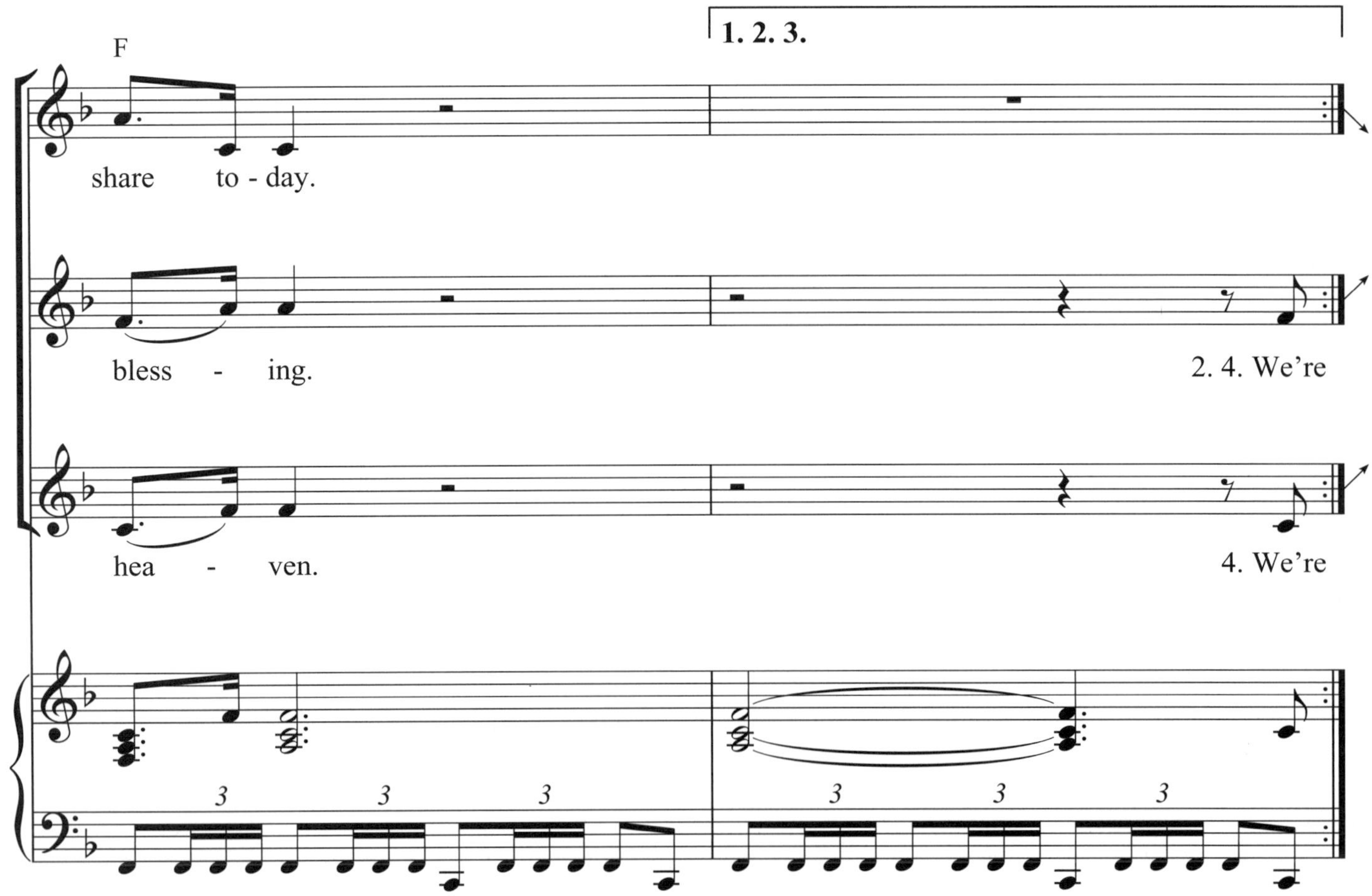
F
1. 2. 3.
share to - day.
bless - ing. 2. 4. We're
hea - ven. 4. We're
3 3 3 3 3 3

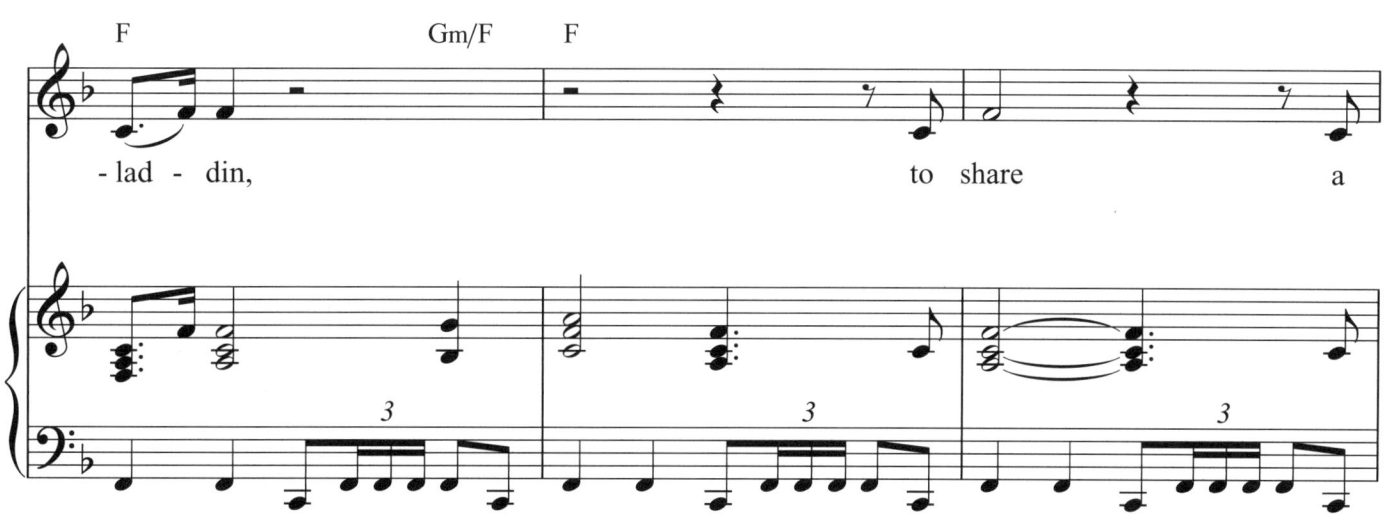

A Panto Like No Other!

Scheherezade: To cheer the gifted cast and crew
Who performed this panto just for you!

Words and Music by
Mark and Helen Johnson

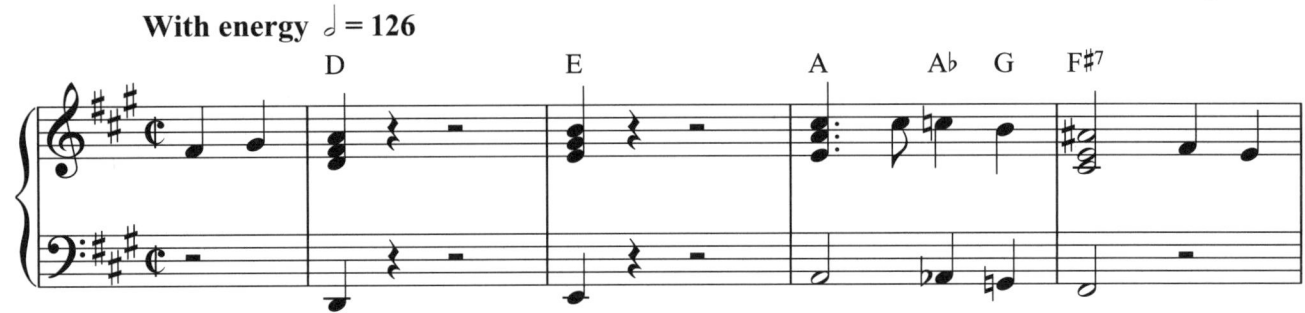

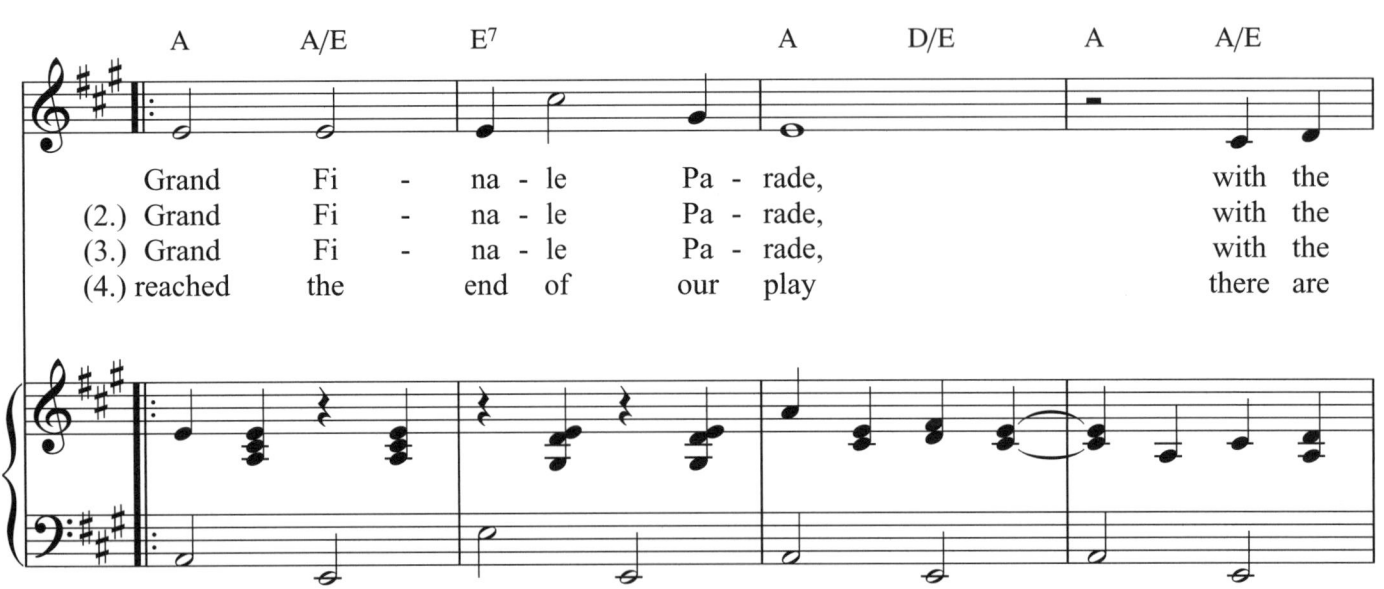

Grand Fi - na - le Pa - rade,   with the
(2.) Grand Fi - na - le Pa - rade,   with the
(3.) Grand Fi - na - le Pa - rade,   with the
(4.) reached the end of our play   there are

© 2014 Out of the Ark Ltd, Middlesex TW12 2HD
CCLI Song No. 7004522

* Replace with 'good day' or 'goodnight' if preferred.

Aladdin Refrain

SFX Loud Gong

1. Aladdin, Aladdin, you've got no idea of all that's waiting to happen,
   Aladdin, Aladdin, we'll be here to cheer you all the way.
   Aladdin, Aladdin, you've got no idea of all that's waiting to happen,
   Aladdin, Aladdin, hope you're going to keep us entertained!

Wantu: Abanazar will just use him and then leave him in the lurch!

2. Aladdin, Aladdin, who's the lovely lady that has taken your fancy?
   Aladdin, Aladdin, did you think to ask her for her name?
   Aladdin, Aladdin, who's the lovely lady that has taken your fancy?
   Aladdin, Aladdin, bet you'd like to be with her again!

Abanazar: When I come back, he'll be begging me to take the lamp off him – ha, ha, ha!

3. Aladdin, Aladdin, looks like Abanazar's gone and left you abandoned,
   Aladdin, Aladdin, well and truly stuck inside the cave.
   Aladdin, Aladdin, looks like Abanazar's gone and left you abandoned,
   Aladdin, Aladdin, hope you had no other plans today!

Start of Act Two.

4. Aladdin, Aladdin, now you've got the ring, you'll be proposing to Jasmine,
   Aladdin, Aladdin, don't let anything get in the way.
   Aladdin, Aladdin, now you've got the ring, you'll be proposing to Jasmine,
   Aladdin, Aladdin, all you've got to do is name the day!

Abanazar: I can afford a professional now, like (Alastair Campbell). Go on, shoo!

5. Aladdin, Aladdin, just when things were better than you'd ever imagined,
   Aladdin, Aladdin, seems your luck's run out on you again.
   Aladdin, Aladdin, just when things were better than you'd ever imagined,
   Aladdin, Aladdin, is this where the story has to end?

Words and Music by Mark and Helen Johnson
© 2014 Out of the Ark Ltd, Middlesex TW12 2HD
CCLI Song No. 7004518

In The Marketplace

Villager 4: I'll have ten metres for my wife!
Wife: Oi! Don't be cheeky, you distant cousin of a gnat!

1. Off to market with my basket,
    On my way.
    Finest veggies, ripe and ready,
    Here today.
    Herbs and spices, all great prices,
    Don't delay.
    Another day in the marketplace.

2. Hustle, bustle, people shuffle
    On their way.
    Chitter, chatter, friendly natter,
    Lots to say.
    Buying, selling, there's no telling
    What you'll pay.
    Another day in the marketplace.

    CHORUS   *Everywhere you go*
    There are plenty of people passing through.
    Some are sure to be out for a wallet or two!
    Everywhere you go
    There are plenty of treasures on display.
    Just be sure to watch out as you go on your way!

3. Eastern dancers, sounds of laughter
    Fill the day.
    Flutes and shakers, music-makers,
    Hear them play.
    Carpet-sellers, story-tellers,
    Be amazed.
    Another day in the marketplace.

    CHORUS

    Repeat verse 2

    CHORUS

Words and Music by Mark and Helen Johnson
© 2014 Out of the Ark Ltd, Middlesex TW12 2HD
CCLI Song No. 7004525

I've Had Enough

Maid 1: Don't be too keen to give up being royal, being ordinary's not all that!

JASMINE
1. I've had enough of all their expectations,
   I'm sick of all the royal regulations,
   A crazy rule to spoil it all – it makes no sense to me.

JASMINE and MAIDS
2. I must have seen at least a hundred princes,
   A thousand more and still you'd not convince me.
   I can't pretend, 'cos none of them would be the best for me.

CHORUS
JASMINE & ALL
I've lived a life of luxury,
But now it doesn't mean that much to me –
That's not who I am.
There's so much more I want to see
And choices only I can make for me –
Can't they understand,
JASMINE
I need to be who I am?

JASMINE
3. A palace life is one of limitations,
   The world outside is full of fascination,
   With air to breathe, a life to lead that I can call my own.

JASMINE and MAIDS
4. If this is what it means to be a princess,
   I think it's fair to say I'm losing interest.
   There's so much more beyond these walls that I am yet to see.

CHORUS

Repeat verses 1 and 2 (ALL)

CHORUS
I've lived a life of luxury,
But now it doesn't mean that much to me –
That's not who I am.
There's so much more I want to see
And choices only I can make for me –
Can't they understand?
There's so much more I want to see
And choices only I can make for me –
Can't they understand,
JASMINE
I need to be who I am?

Words and Music by Mark and Helen Johnson
© 2014 Out of the Ark Ltd, Middlesex TW12 2HD
CCLI Song No. 7004523

Some Things Go Together Perfectly

Jasmine: *A tickled onion!*
Aladdin: *Hey, we could be a double act!*

ALADDIN
1 Hey! It never occurred to me
How easy a day could be,
But you have made it better, by far!
JASMINE
Say! It certainly seemed to me
You needed some company,
It's truly been a pleasure, so far!

CHORUS
ALL
Bangers and mash,
Carrots and peas,
Need one another like a cracker needs cheese.
Bacon and eggs,
Strawberries and cream,
Some things go together perfectly!

ALADDIN – an aside
2 Wow! There's something about her smile,
A girl with a certain style, and how
I'm glad I've met her, yes sir!
My! She's taken me by surprise,
The moment I saw those eyes, and now
I can't forget her, no sir!

CHORUS (ALL)

JASMINE – an aside
3 Boy! It's such an amazing day,
I don't even know his name, but WOW,
I'm glad I met him – drop jaw!
He's a likeable kind of guy,
It's hit me between the eyes, and now
I won't forget him, for sure!

CHORUS x 2 (ALL)
ALADDIN & JASMINE
Some things go together perfectly!

Words and Music by Mark and Helen Johnson
© 2014 Out of the Ark Ltd, Middlesex TW12 2HD
CCLI Song No. 7004529

Just Three Wishes

Genie: Look, why don't you just sit here and we'll go over it in our own, unique style!

CHORUS
*Just three wishes
Can make your dreams reality,
The sky's the limit, I've seen it all before!
Just three wishes,
You've gone and won the lottery,
But one condition: don't ask for any more!*

GENIE
1 Everything you've always wanted, anything you ask,
Nothing is too difficult, your wish is my command.
If it's other people, some restrictions may apply,
I won't make them fall in love or bring them back to life!
THE THREE WISHES
(Back to life, back to life!)

CHORUS *(ALL)*

GENIE and THE THREE WISHES
2 I could make you rich and famous, eloquent and wise,
Give you superhuman powers, teach you how to fly.
You could move a mountain, have a picnic on the moon,
You can ask for anything to make your dreams come true!
THE THREE WISHES
(Dreams come true, dreams come true!)

ALL
Repeat song

CHORUS x 2

Words and Music by Mark and Helen Johnson
© 2014 Out of the Ark Ltd, Middlesex TW12 2HD
CCLI Song No. 7004537

New Lamps For Old

Abanazar: New lamps for old! Think Ikea – out with the old, in with the new!

(To be sung as a 3-part song)

ABANAZAR

1. New lamps for old! New lamps for old!
   Bring me your rubbish, I'll turn it to gold!
   Tell everyone what you've been told,
   I'll give you new lamps for old!
   (Repeat with ABANAZAR and GROUP 1)

ABANAZAR

2. Out with your copper and out with your bronze!
   (This special offer can't last very long.)
   Don't take my word for it, try one today,
   Think of the pennies you'll save!
   (Repeat with ABANAZAR and GROUP 2)

Sing verse 1 (ABANAZAR) with verse 2 (GROUP 2)

ABANAZAR

3. Come on you ladies, you've nothing to lose!
   These lamps are tested and fully approved.
   Quality lighting to meet every need,
   All with a year's guarantee!
   (Repeat with ABANAZAR and GROUP 3)

Sing verse 2 (GROUP 2) with verse 3 (GROUP 3)

Sing verse 1 (GROUP 1) with verse 2 (GROUP 2) and verse 3 (GROUP 3)

Repeat verse 1 (ABANAZAR)

Words and Music by Mark and Helen Johnson
© 2014 Out of the Ark Ltd, Middlesex TW12 2HD
CCLI Song No. 7004526

Wishy Washy Laun-d-ry

Widow T: I can see it all now, we'll be just like 'Glossy Goss' magazine. All the celebs will bring their dirty laundry to us!

CHORUS
*Working your socks off?
Feeling you've not stopped?
Tired of never getting all the help you need?
You can be free!
Time to try your Wishy Washy Laun-d-ry.
Bring us your troubles,
We've got the bubbles!
Widow Twankey's got herself a new machine –
Cleans like a dream!
Gets your washing whiter than you've ever seen!*

1. Mondays through to Fridays,
   Every day's a 'wash 'n' dry' day,
   We're the best in town, (best in town).
   Leave us all your dirties,
   'Cause we're here from seven thirty
   And we never hang around!

   CHORUS

2. You will not alarm us
   With your polka-dot pyjamas,
   'Cause we've seen it all, (seen it all).
   Lingerie and bloomers
   That could start a thousand rumours,
   But we're too professional!

   CHORUS

3. Bring your suits and dresses,
   When we get them on the presses
   They'll be good as new, (good as new).
   No one does it better
   Than your local launderette-a,
   Not from here to Timbuktu!

   CHORUS *(Repeat last line)*

Words and Music by Mark and Helen Johnson
© 2014 Out of the Ark Ltd, Middlesex TW12 2HD
CCLI Song No. 7004536

I Still Believe

Aladdin: I really thought we...
Jasmine: ...were meant to be together for ever.

      JASMINE
1   Who'd have thought that life would come to this
    When we sealed our future with a kiss?
    Who'd have thought that everything could change so painfully?
    ALADDIN
    From the day we said our first 'hello'
    I knew then I couldn't let you go.
    Was it so impossible, the thought of you and me?

                  ALADDIN and JASMINE
CHORUS   *I need to find how to keep hope alive,*
                  Putting my fears aside and holding on.
                  I still believe something inside of me
                  Knows we were meant to be and live as one.

      JASMINE and GIRLS
2   Who'd have thought I'd be in such a place?
    How I wish that I could see your face,
    Just the thought of losing you is tearing me apart.
    ALADDIN and BOYS
    If I thought there's something I could do,
    You know I'd do anything for you,
    But it seems impossible, I don't know where to start!

                  ALL
BRIDGE   All our longing turned to nothing,
                  How could things so wonderful be lost in just a day?
                  All our dreaming and believing,
                  Everything we talked about has all been snatched away.

BRIDGE *(ALL)* and CHORUS *(ALADDIN and JASMINE)*

Repeat verse 1 (ALADDIN and JASMINE)

Words and Music by Mark and Helen Johnson
© 2014 Out of the Ark Ltd, Middlesex TW12 2HD
CCLI Song No. 7004520

The Chase

Aladdin: You should have a word with my mum! Let's see if we can find her!

GROUP 1: WIDOW TWANKEY, WISHY, WASHY

1. Time to tiptoe out of here, out of here, out of here,
Find a way to disappear before they catch us up!
(Repeat)

GROUP 2: ABANAZAR and GUARDS

2. Mustn't let them get away, get away, get away,
Find the lamp without delay, got to keep up!
(Repeat)

GROUP 3: ALADDIN, JASMINE and KING

3. Think I saw them over there, over there, over there,
I'd know that shape anywhere! Oh what a stroke of luck!
(Repeat)

GROUP 1

4. Hurry now, they're catching up, catching up, catching up.
(WT to audience)
Tell you what, I've had enough of running round this stage!
(Repeat)

GROUP 2

5. When I get my hands on her, hands on her, hands on her,
Then my evil plans will turn matters my way!
(Repeat)

GROUP 3

6. I can see she's got the lamp, got the lamp, got the lamp,
Not so sure she's got the stamina to get away!
(Repeat)

GROUP 1

7. Can't keep going any more, any more, any more,
My poor feet are very sore, I put it down to age.
(Repeat)
(Group freeze on spot, pose as trees/statues)

GROUP 2

8. Did we come this way before, way before, way before?
Something looks 'famili-or' here in this place!
(Repeat)

GROUP 3

9   Widow Twankey! Rub the lamp! Rub the lamp! Rub the lamp!
    Free the Genie while you can, and then we'll all be saved!
    (Repeat)

WIDOW TWANKEY

10 Are you saying 'Rob a bank! Rob a bank! Rob a bank!'?
    Why would I be doing that? You must think I'm insane!
    (Repeat)

GROUP 3

11 Widow Twankey! Rub the lamp! Rub the lamp! Rub the lamp!
    (Aside to the audience)
    You'll have everybody's thanks saving the day!
    (Repeat)

GROUP 2

12 That's enough of silly pranks, silly pranks, silly pranks,
    I will have Aladdin's lamp, no matter what you say!
    (Repeat)

ALL
BOO! HISS!
BOO! HISS!

ABANAZAR
I will have Aladdin's lamp, no matter what you say!

ALL
BOO! HISS!
BOO! HISS!

ABANAZAR
I will have Aladdin's lamp, no matter what you say!
(Evil laugh)

WIDOW TWANKEY
CATCH!

Words by Mark and Helen Johnson
Music based on a theme from *Peer Gynt Suite No.1* by Edvard Grieg, adapted by Mark and Helen Johnson
© 2014 Out of the Ark Ltd, Middlesex TW12 2HD
CCLI Song No. 7004532

Wedding Procession

MC: *Would you all please rise!*

(To be sung in 3 parts.)

GROUP 1
1. We're here for Jasmine and Aladdin,
   To share a marriage made in heaven.

GROUP 2
2. We're here to celebrate this wedding,
   To share this joyful day of blessing.

GROUP 3
3. We are here to share in the joys of this, their wedding day.
   Many years, they've waited to find the love they share today.

4. *Sing all verses together in harmony*

5. We're here for Jasmine and Aladdin,
   To share a marriage made in heaven.

Words and Music by Mark and Helen Johnson
© 2014 Out of the Ark Ltd, Middlesex TW12 2HD
CCLI Song No. 7004535

A Panto Like No Other!

Scheherazade: To cheer the gifted cast and crew
Who performed this panto just for you!

1. It's a Grand Finale Parade,
   With the cast all gathered on stage.
   Now the genie's found his freedom,
   Abanazar's met his match,
   And Widow Twankey's got herself a rather handsome chap!

   CHORUS   *It's a Grand Finale Parade,*
   We hope you're glad you came.
   We've had fun too, entertaining you
   In a panto like no other today!

2. It's a Grand Finale Parade,
   With the cast all gathered on stage.
   It's the perfect happy ending
   To a complicated plot,
   The village hall was opened and Aladdin tied the knot!

   CHORUS

3. It's a Grand Finale Parade,
   With the cast all gathered on stage.
   There's been lots of fun and laughter
   And we've heard you boo and clap,
   And now we'd like to hear the sound of money in the hat!

   CHORUS

4. Now we've reached the end of our play
   There are 'thank you's we have to say:
   For the scenery and make-up;
   For the costumes and the props;
   For all the lovely teachers who have pulled out all the stops!

   CHORUS   *It's a Grand Finale Parade,*
   We hope you're glad you came.
   We've had fun too, entertaining you
   In a panto like no other,
   A panto like no other,
   A panto like no other today!
   Thank you for coming, goodbye!*

*Replace with 'good day' or 'goodnight' if preferred.

Words and Music by Mark and Helen Johnson
© 2014 Out of the Ark Ltd, Middlesex TW12 2HD
CCLI Song No. 7004522

LET ME TELL YOU A STORY

> The night wrapped around you is inky black. You shuffle on your bottom as close as you dare to the blazing fire, its mischievous flickerings sending shadows leaping and dancing into the trees. Grandmother lifts her wrinkled face, gazes deep into the flames and begins her story...

Who would like to be a Scheherazade?

There are lots of fun activities that can help people of all ages learn to be effective storytellers. The necessary skills are not only useful when performing, but are beneficial in many areas of life, as they will equip you to become a good communicator. So, building confidence and competence in speaking out loud and developing a capacity for active listening are definitely desirable outcomes, (not to mention ticking some boxes on the new Literacy curriculum 2014).

The following is really just a 'starter pack' but will hopefully whet your appetite to find out more!

Storytelling is as old as language itself. Before writing was developed, stories were passed down orally. This is how communities kept alive their history, culture and religion. Myths and legends were developed to help people come to terms with the world around them, much of which could not yet be understood on a scientific basis. Many of these myths and legends still survive today, often because they were designed to carry a universal truth, such as the battle between good and evil which is experienced by each of us on different levels.

A story which is told, rather than read, is a living thing – changing with every telling. The main characters and plot outline remain the same but each person telling the story tells it differently, responding to their audience, perhaps adding a joke that suddenly occurs to them or making a connection between the story and the audience. This is both the scariest and most thrilling aspect of being a storyteller!

Beginning the journey...

Give children one line of a well-known nursery rhyme or poem. Ask them to move around the space and, whenever you clap, to repeat the line to the person closest to them, each time saying it in a different way e.g. as though you are in an argument/as though it's a secret/as if you're giving an order/as though it's the punchline to a joke/as if you're underwater, and so on. Offer lots of suggestions, but let them choose each time so that not everybody is doing the same thing at the same time. This will help make them aware of their vocal range.

Encourage projection (not shouting) by having pairs face each other with some distance between them. Tell them that even though there will be several people talking at once, they need to communicate to their partner what they had for breakfast/what their favourite TV programme is, etc. Remind them where their diaphragm is and ask them to place their hand over it and feel the movement as they take in a deep breath (making sure they keep their shoulders still) and practice 'pushing' their voice from there.

Winking Murder

This popular game will help children practise making eye contact. The basic rules are: children sit in a circle; someone goes out and the rest of the group decide who will be the murderer; the murderer murders by winking at people and they die in as loud and dramatic a way as possible; the person who has been sent out re-enters before the killing begins and has to guess who the murderer is by spotting them winking.

Remembering story sequences

The following activities will help children discover ways of remembering the sequence of a story.

Divide into groups of 5 or 6. Give each group a simple, well-known story. As a group, they must decide the 4 or 5 main plot points and for each one produce a 'frozen' picture or tableau. One of the children then tells the story (without a script), as it is illustrated by the tableau – each part of the story could be told by different children. Show to the other groups and, if possible, revisit each one at a chosen point and ask the audience to add some exciting vocabulary.

Alternatively, have the group draw a story path or mind map using visual symbols to act as prompts for them to tell the story. These are not illustrations to be held up, but rather visual prompts for the tellers.

The leader reads a story. When everyone is seated in a circle, it is then re-read (or told) and whenever a person or inanimate object is mentioned, someone moves into the centre of the circle and 'becomes' that person or object. (You will need to decide if they should move or remain still.) This continues and the picture builds up until you say 'Whoosh!' and everyone must return to their place and you can carry on with different children then taking part.

Developing Improvisation Skills

Try using the scaffolding of a fortunately/unfortunately activity. For example, with a new person starting each line, they might say:

- Fortunately we went on holiday last week.
- Unfortunately, it rained all week.
- Fortunately, we were in a weatherproof dome.
- Unfortunately, it developed a huge crack.

Each person must accept what the previous person has said and build on it and not go off at inappropriate tangents. Useful for developing listening and turn-taking skills.

Develop vocabulary by having a bag full of words which are picked out at random. The picker then tries to think of two other words which could be used instead, for example 'road' could be substituted with 'path' or 'highway'. Allow 'phone a friend' to help children who might find this difficult.

Simply encourage the children in pairs to tell each other a favourite family story or a story which is/was one of their favourites.

Do you think there might be a story that is looking for you?

> 'Australian Aborigines say that the big stories – the stories worth telling and retelling, the ones in which you may find the meaning of your life – are forever stalking the right teller, sniffing and tracking like predators hunting their prey in the bush.'
>
> Robert Moss

Licence Application Form
(Aladdin Trouble)

If you perform *Aladdin Trouble* to an audience other than children and staff you will need to photocopy and complete this form and return it by post or fax to Out of the Ark Music in order to apply for a licence. If anticipated audience sizes are very small or if special circumstances apply please contact Out of the Ark Music.

The licence will permit the holder to:
- Perform *Aladdin Trouble* on the dates applied for.
- Reproduce the lyrics to the songs on printed paper, such as for programmes, and to make transparencies for overhead projection. The following credit should be included: 'Reproduced by kind permission © Out of the Ark Ltd'.
- Photocopy the script for learning purposes. Copies must be destroyed after the performance.
- Make no more than two copies of the music, to be used by participating musicians on the performance dates.

If the performance is to be recorded please contact Out of the Ark Music.

We wish to apply for a licence to perform *Aladdin Trouble* by Mark and Helen Johnson

Customer number (if known): ....

Name of school / organisation: ....

Name of organiser / producer: ....

Date(s) of performance(s): ....

Invoice address: ....

....

Post code: ....   Country: ....

Telephone number: ....

Number of performances (excl. dress rehearsal)	Performances without admission charges*	Performances with admission charges*
1	☐ £24.00 [€31.25]	☐ £30.64 [€39.85]
2	☐ £30.64 [€39.85]	☐ £40.85 [€53.10]
3 or more	☐ £40.85 [€53.10]	☐ £51.06 [€66.40]

Tick one of the boxes above.

☐ Tick here to receive licensing information for any audio or video recording of a performance.

Tick one of the four payment options below: (Invoices will be sent with all licences)

☐ Please bill my school/nursery at the above address (UK schools/nurseries only)

☐ I enclose a cheque (Pounds Sterling) for £ .... payable to Out of the Ark Music

☐ I enclose a cheque (Euro) for € .... payable to Out of the Ark Music

☐ Please charge the following card: (Visa [not Electron], MasterCard & Maestro accepted)

Card No ....

Start Date _ _ / _ _ (MM/YY)   Expiry Date _ _ / _ _ (MM/YY)   3 digit security code: _ _ _ (last 3 digits on signature strip)

Address:	Out of the Ark Music Kingsway Business Park Oldfield Road Hampton Middlesex TW12 2HD United Kingdom	Phone: Fax: Email:	+44 (0)20 8481 7200 +44 (0)20 8941 5548 info@outoftheark.com

*The licence fees shown on this form are for 2014-2015 and include VAT at 20%. Prices may be subject to revision. Customers outside the EU will NOT be charged VAT.